Featherstone

CREATIVE PLANNING IN THE EYFS

Castles and Dragons

Lucy Peet

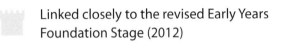

- Linked closely to the revised Early Years Foundation Stage (2012)

- Six weeks of differentiated planning

- Coverage across the 7 areas and 17 aspects of learning

- Activities based upon Playing and Exploring, Active Learning, Creating and Thinking Critically

- Guidance on assessing characterisitics of learning

Published 2012 by Featherstone Education
Bloomsbury Publishing Plc
50 Bedford Square, London, WC1B 3DP
www.bloomsbury.com

ISBN 978-1-4081-7393-0

Text © Lucy Peet 2012
Design © Lynda Murray
Photographs © Shutterstock

Printed in Great Britain by Latimer Trend & Company Ltd

10 9 8 7 6 5 4 3 2 1

This book is produced using paper that is made from wood grown in
managed, sustainable forests. It is natural, renewable and recyclable.
The logging and manufacturing processes conform to the environmental
regulations of the country of origin.

To see our full range of titles visit www.bloomsbury.com

Contents

Introduction to the series...4

The revised curriculum...6

Effective learning, observation and assessment...8

Week 1: **Castles and houses**...10

Week 2: **Armour and battles**...18

Week 3: **Dangerous dragons!**...26

Week 4: **Knight journeys**...34

Week 5: **Kings and queens**...42

Week 6: **A grand banquet!**...50

Learning characteristics...57

Group record sheets...58

Planning overview...62

Introduction

About the series

This book is part of a series written for all who work with children in the Foundation Stage (FS). Owing to the fun, practical nature of the activities it is suitable for a wide range of settings, including schools, pre-schools, childminders and nurseries. Given that all the activities are differentiated for children working towards the Early Learning Goals (ELGs) 'the knowledge, skills and understanding children should have at the end of the academic year in which they turn five' (p.2, 2012), it is particularly relevant to practitioners working with FS1, FS2 and mixed-age classes. However, with the increasing good practice of the FS extending into Year 1 and 2 this book is invaluable for teachers wishing to promote active learning and a creative curriculum with children up to the age of seven. Each activity links with the requirements and expectations of the National Curriculum, statutory for Key Stage 1 in England and Wales, and through observation it will also be possible to collect evidence for Assessing Pupils' Progress. The table below shows the corresponding year groups for children from Scotland and Northern Ireland.

Year groups and corresponding ages:

Age	School year		
	England and Wales	**Scotland**	**Northern Ireland**
2 - 3	Foundation Stage		
3 - 4	FS1 (previously nursery)		P 1
4 - 5	FS2 (previously reception)	Primary 1	P 2
5 - 6	Year 1	Primary 2	P 3
6 - 7	Year 2	Primary 3	P 4

How this book is structured

Through the topic of castles children will be involved in playing and exploring, active learning and creating and thinking critically: all key features of the revised Early Years Foundation Stage (EYFS) (2012). This book contains six weeks of planning – five weeks of detailed plans, with an activity designed for each specific area of learning, and a celebratory week of activity to share with parents and carers at the end covering the 'prime areas of learning'. Details are shown in the six week planning overview grid on page 62.

Activities are structured to build upon children's skills over the six weeks developing their experiences and abilities. For example, week 1 introduces a mathematical shape activity where the children build castles and houses using 3D shapes. They will measure, cut, shape and join where appropriate. These skills are continued and extended in week 2 when they build a working catapult from junk modelling and measure the distance a missile can be flung! The story of Rapunzel is explored in week one when the children make puppets from lolly sticks and act out the story. The story is further consolidated in week 3 when they make a board game similar to snakes and ladders based upon the story of Rapunzel, where the players climb up Rapunzel's hair.

Through this method of extending similar tasks at a later date children are able to consolidate their knowledge and practise their skills. The final week of celebration through a grand banquet is an opportunity to share the topic with parents and carers.

Each activity is clearly structured, with suggestions for:

◆ Resources required with relevant storybook or non-fiction book suggestions to support the main idea

◆ Key vocabulary

◆ A simple 'what to do' explanation with ideas for both guided and independent activity

◆ Differentiation of the activity at three levels. Each activity is pitched at an average level of understanding in line with the expected level of the ELGs. There are also ideas to **support** children who are working at the emerging stage and to **extend** children who are exceeding the ELGs. This clear differentiation ensures that all children in the group are exploring new ideas and concepts at a level appropriate to their stage of development. The Statutory Framework for the Early Years Foundation Stage states that (p.11) 'Practitioners must indicate whether children are meeting expected levels of development, or if they are exceeding expected levels, or not yet reaching expected levels. This is the EYFS Profile. The extension activities in this book are planned in line with the National Curriculum, ensuring that the children are building a firm foundation for Years 1 and 2.

◆ How to extend the activity throughout the week, with suggestions on how to deliver the activity as a **guided** session and ideas on how to encourage the children to work **independently**. The Statutory Framework for the Early Years Foundation Stage recognises that there is an important balance between activities led by children and activities led or guided by adults. It is important that 'each area of learning and development must be implemented through planned, purposeful play and through a mix of adult-led and child-initiated activity' (p.6, 2012). Each activity in this book includes guidance for practitioners as to how this balance can be achieved.

◆ Ideas for interactive display within the setting

◆ Ideas for parents and carers to use at home

Parents and carers as partners

Parents and carers are crucial in developing and supporting children's learning. This is recognised in the revised EYFS, and a key recommendation from the Tickell Review is that (p.18) '...the Government increases the emphasis within the EYFS on the role of parents and carers as partners in their children's learning...'. Indeed, the *Statutory Framework for the Early Years Foundation Stage* (March 2012) states that (p.2) 'Good parenting and high quality early learning together provide the foundation children need to make the most of their abilities and talents as they grow up'. The planning in this book includes an entire week based around inviting parents and carers into the setting to share in their children's curiosity and enthusiasm for learning. There are examples of how parents and carers can extend the learning at home, and ideas for giving parents and carers the opportunity not only to see what activities their children have been involved in, but also for them to join in alongside their children and to be really 'hands on'! One of the features which the EYFS seeks to provide (p.2, 2012) is 'partnership working between practitioners and with parents and/or carers'. This book recognises this as a priority.

Outdoor learning

Most of the activities are more than suitable to be engaged with outdoors as well as in a classroom – indeed for some of the activities it is necessary to be outdoors! And for some very messy, noisy or extensive activities I would recommend setting up outdoors to save carpets and soft furnishings and to minimise disruption to the rest of the learning environment. Hardly any of the activities require the children to sit and write in a formal situation. Where there is a suggestion to record, it is done either by an adult on a flipchart, children on individual whiteboards or pictorially, or through ICT, for example by the children using a digital camera or making a sound recording.

The revised curriculum

It is four years since the EYFS was introduced to provide a framework for all children in early years settings. The Tickell Report (2011) was carried out as an evaluation of the EYFS on children's outcomes and on those people working in the early years. One of the recommendations from the Tickell Report (2011) was that…

> …the assessment at the end of the EYFS, the EYFS Profile, should be significantly slimmed down and made much more manageable, based upon [my] 17 proposed new early learning goals…

The themes, principles and commitments of the EYFS remain the same, however the fourth theme, Learning and development has changed. This is the focus of our *Creative Planning in the EYFS* series. The *Statutory Framework for the Early Years Foundation Stage* (March 2012) states that one of the overarching principles which should shape practice in early years settings (p.3) is that 'children develop and learn in different ways and at different rates.' This book shows how topic-based activities can be provided in an exciting and practical way whilst still offering opportunities for all children at three levels of differentiation.

The research studied for the Tickell Report (2011) focuses on the concept that some aspects of development and learning include developing abilities, enabling children to be successful in all areas. These are referred to as 'prime areas of learning' and development. Other areas of learning are more specific to areas of knowledge and skills, these are known as 'specific areas of learning and development'.

Prime areas of learning and development

1. Communication and language

2. Physical development

3. Personal, social and emotional development

Specific areas of learning and development

1. Literacy

2. Mathematics

3. Understanding the world

4. Expressive arts and design

The activities in this book are planned around the four specific areas of learning and development – Literacy (formerly Communication, Language and Literacy), Mathematics (formerly Problem Solving, Reasoning and Numeracy), Understanding the world (formerly Knowledge and Understanding of the world) and Expressive Arts and Design (formerly Creative Development). However, the three prime areas are also covered through discussion, speaking and listening, turn taking and involvement in each task. It is essential that the prime and specific areas are planned for and experienced at the same time. They are not to be experienced chronologically but as an interwoven fabric of early years provision, as 'all areas of learning and development are important and inter-connected' (p.4, 2012).

Development in the prime areas has been called by neuroscientists 'experience expectant learning'. This is where a child's brain is ready to respond to interaction and stimulus, developing connections. Development in the specific areas however, will only develop when the need occurs, and includes cultural concepts such as learning to read and write, understand numbers, the number system and maps. This has been referred to as 'experience dependent learning'. (Hall, 2005).

The revisions made in the EYFS separate out the four strands of speaking, listening, reading and writing identified in the Rose Review (2006) into two areas: Communication and language (prime area) and Literacy (specific area). The Tickell Report (2011) explains this:

> ...the development of communication and language skills happens during an optimum window of brain development and is experience expectant (therefore...prime)...whereas the acquisition of literacy skills is experience dependent since it can occur at any point in childhood or adulthood. (p.98)

As communication, language and literacy is so inextricably linked I have used ELGs from both these areas in the detailed differentiated activities.

Further reading

Hall, John (February 2005) **Neuroscience and Education – A review of the contribution of brain science to teaching and learning** *Research Report No.121* Scottish Council for Research in Education

Rose, Jim (March 2006) **Independent review of the teaching of early reading** *Final report* Department for Education and Skills

Tickell, Clare (March 2011) **The Early Years: Foundations for life, health and learning** – An Independent Report on the Early Years Foundation Stage to Her Majesty's Government

Department for Education (March 2012) **Statutory Framework for the Early Years Foundation Stage** – Setting the standards for learning, development and care for children from birth to five

Effective learning, observation and assessment

Characteristics of Effective Learning

There are a number of learning characteristics which are evident in all seven areas of learning and development (p.7, 2012). These are not sequential, and it is not possible to identify particular ages or stages when they may be achieved. Learning characteristics include:

- **Playing and exploring** – engagement

- **Active learning** – motivation

- **Creating and thinking critically** – thinking

These learning characteristics should not be considered as an outcome which is summative, or marked in a 'tick list' manner. They represent processes, and may be observed during formative assessment.

Observation

It is crucial to observe children during their participation in these activities in order to assess whether they are working at an appropriate level and to work out their next steps in learning. The differentiation planned in the activity provides suitable challenge for all children.

Children can behave very differently during group, guided, independent and one-to-one opportunities. Some may be very quiet, and appear withdrawn or insecure during a group activity. However, given the opportunity to work with a close friend independently or at a self-chosen activity, a far more confident child may become apparent. Regular observation should therefore be a central part of good early years practice, ensuring that children are observed during different types of activity (guided, shared, self-chosen or independent), in differently sized groups with a range of children and at different times of day.

Sometimes it is useful to have a focus for observation such as an area of development or to discover the style of a child's learning, but at other times it is just as useful to observe the child for a period of time simply to discover what they are all about. If it appears that the child is making good progress, and is able to achieve what is required in an activity it is important to be aware of their next steps in learning. By always providing an opportunity for children to extend their learning they will continue to be interested and motivated, enjoying learning and finding out about new ideas. All of these are valuable personal characteristics which will be necessary throughout the whole of a child's life.

Assessment

The new EYFS will expect practicioners to make judgements as to whether a child is meeting, exceeding or emerging in relation to the Early Learning Goals (ELGs). In addition to their judgements, practicioners will need to make an assessment against the 3 characterisitcs of effective learning (see Observation record sheet page 57). As previously discussed, a child's learning characteristics are not suitable for summative assessment in a 'can they/can't they' manner. Rather, they should be thought of as part of a child's learning journey. It is for this reason that I am not recommending the use of a 'tick list' to record achievement of each learning characteristic. However, a simple observation record could include the characteristics observed during the observation and the context. This would build into a collection of evidence showing each child's strengths and areas for development. An example of an individual observation record of learning characteristics is provided on page 57.

The ELGs in both the prime and specific areas of learning are set at the expected level for a child nearing the end of FS2. Some children may be working towards achieving these goals and some may be exceeding them – it is the nature of any cohort of children. Indeed, there is likely to be discrepancy at times in a child's attainment towards the ELGs between areas of learning – a child rarely makes equal and comparative progress in all areas across a period of a year or more. It is not necessary to record in a numerical manner how a child achieves, but by highlighting the statement which most closely matches the attainment of the child, it is possible to identify their level of understanding and plan the next steps in progressing towards and exceeding the ELGs.

Using the group record sheets

The group record sheets on pages 58-61 can be used to show how a group of children are achieving at any one time – as a snapshot. It does not show progress over time or individual children's next steps but may be useful as a tool to show a co-ordinator or setting leader the strengths and areas for development of a cohort. It is not possible to fit all specific areas of learning onto one sheet so you may need to photocopy some back to back. There are a variety of record sheets here for both specific and prime areas of development. The group record sheet on page 58 for Communication and Language (prime) and Literacy (specific) also gives the opportunity to record achievement in all three areas on the same sheet, as some activities use ELGs from all of these areas. You may choose to use a traffic light system to record where children are in relation to each area of learning.

Castles and houses

Rapunzel, Rapunzel

The children will be reading and listening to the story of Rapunzel and retelling it using props, including a lolly stick character with yellow ribbon hair.

Resources

* Film or cartoon of Rapunzel

* Simple sound recording of the story

* Role-play clothes or props for Rapunzel, the Prince and the Wicked Witch

* Flipchart

* Lolly sticks

* Yellow ribbon

* Gold paper scraps

* Scraps of fabric

* Glue stick

* Sticky labels

Storybooks

* *Rapunzel* by The Brothers Grimm (many versions of this traditional tale such as Ladybird)

Key vocabulary

* Rapunzel
* Wicked Witch
* Prince
* tower
* hair
* puppet
* character
* setting

Observation and assessment

Communication and Language	Expected statements (ELGs)
Listening and attention	Children listen attentively in a range of situations. They listen to stories, accurately anticipating key events and respond to what they hear with relevant comments, questions or actions.
Speaking	Children express themselves effectively, showing awareness of listeners' needs. They use past, present and future forms accurately when talking about events that have happened or are to happen in the future. They develop their own narratives and explanations by connecting ideas or events.

Literacy	Expected statements (ELGs)
Reading	Children read and understand simple sentences. They use phonic knowledge to decode regular words and read them aloud accurately. They also read some common irregular words. They demonstrate understanding when talking with others about what they have read.

What to do

Read the traditional tale of Rapunzel. Look at several different versions if possible, including a film or cartoon version. Discuss with the children what was the same and what was different about each version, introducing the key vocabulary and ensuring that the children know the characters' names. Make a simple list on the flipchart of the main characters that appeared in all versions of the story. Talk about the nature of these characters: were they good or bad natured? Talk about the distinguishing features of the characters – if they were puppets how would the children know which were which? Explain to the children that they are going to make some simple lolly stick puppets to represent the main character in the story. Show the children the resources and demonstrate folding over a sticky label onto the top of a lolly stick, sticking it to itself. Draw on Rapunzel's face and wrap a piece of fabric around the lolly stick to represent a clothed body, gluing with a glue stick. Discuss with the children what makes Rapunzel distinctive – what is missing from the puppet? Add on the long yellow ribbon for Rapunzel's hair, showing the children how to measure it against the lolly stick to ensure it is longer than the body.

Tell the story of Rapunzel again in a simple manner, encouraging all the children to join in with their puppets at the appropriate moments. They could hold their puppet high to represent the tower, and drop down the ribbon when the prince says, 'Rapunzel, Rapunzel, let down your hair!'

If this is to be a guided activity…

…then the children can work together with an adult to create their own puppets representing the characters from the story. Encourage them to look at the scraps of fabric and choose colours and textures suitable to make the prince and the wicked witch – maybe add a gold crown to the prince or a black cloak and a mean expression to the witch! Tell the story again, so that the children can join in with their characters.

If this is to be an independent activity…

…then show the children where the collection of objects to make the puppets are and let them retell the story when they have made them. Provide a recording of the story so that the children can listen to it and act with their puppets at the same time. Put out three props or items of clothing for the children to wear when acting out the story, e.g. a headband with a long yellow ribbon attached, a crown and a witches' hat or cloak. Let the children take turns to play the different characters – many of the girls will love to be the prince, and the boys Rapunzel!

To support or extend

To support, have the lolly sticks already prepared with the stickers and clothing attached so that the children simply have to add the ribbon hair and draw a face. Encourage them to use the correct vocabulary when describing the character and talking about the relative length of her hair – long, longer, longest.

To extend, put out the box modelling resources so that the children can work together to create the setting for the story. Help them to roll paper into a tube to make the tower and cut a window for their Rapunzel puppet to poke out of. Make a film of them acting out the story for the children to watch together later.

Ideas for interactive display

- Create a large display with the puppets made by the children, put up a large tower with a window that the Rapunzels can look through, and make some thorny bushes from twigs and leaves to poke the Prince puppets into. Let the children choose the characters to play with.

- Collect and display different versions of the pictures and photographs of the same characters. For example, in one circle put all the different Rapunzels. What is the same about them and what is different? Talk to the children about which they prefer and why.

Parents and carers as partners

At home, use items such as cardboard tubes, wooden pegs, lolly sticks and old socks to make puppets of your child's favourite characters. Decorate with stickers, felt pens, string and buttons in the style of the character. They do not have to look professional for your child to believe that they represent the characters and to play imaginatively with them. If you have old cereal boxes, cut off the front panel so that your child can draw a 'set background' inside, for the characters to move around in front of.

Castles and houses

Box model castles

The children will be making a castle from 3D box models, and adding moving parts such as a drawbridge and portcullis.

Resources

- ★ Pictures and photographs of castles
- ★ Boxes and junk of different sizes
- ★ Cardboard cones
- ★ Art straws or lolly sticks
- ★ Scissors
- ★ String
- ★ Glue
- ★ Paper fasteners
- ★ Stapler
- ★ Digital camera
- ★ Sticky notes
- ★ 3D wooden shapes

Storybooks and non fiction books

- ★ *See Inside Castles* (Usbourne Flap Books) by Katie Daynes
- ★ *Look Inside a Castle* by Conrad Mason

Key vocabulary

- · box
- · rectangle
- · cone
- · cube
- · tube
- · drawbridge
- · square
- · cylinder
- · portcullis
- · cuboid
- · turret

Observation and assessment

Mathematics	Expected statements (ELGs)
Shape, space and measures	Children use everyday language to talk about size, weight, capacity, position, distance, time and money to compare quantities and objects and to solve problems. They recognise, create and describe patterns. They explore characteristics of everyday objects and shapes and use mathematical language to describe them.

What to do

Show the children the photographs of different castles. Talk about which features are the same and which are different, introducing some of the key vocabulary. Look at the castles non-fiction books to identify specific features (e.g. turrets, drawbridge, portcullis etc.). Ensure that all children know what these parts look like and what they are for.

Demonstrate putting together a castle from boxes, talking about the turrets in the corners and the castle walls. Explain to the children that they can paint and decorate their castle to make it look like it is made from stone.

Talk about the drawbridge and demonstrate how to cut a flap shaped in an arc so that the hinge is at the bottom. Attach a piece of string to each side and to the castle wall so that the door can be lowered down to make a drawbridge, and then folded back into the side of the castle wall.

Show the children how to make a portcullis by laying five or six straws or lolly sticks down with a small gap between each one. Lay five or six more straws or sticks across the others at 90 degrees to the first and glue them down, making a lattice square. Glue a strip of cardboard or a lolly stick to the top of it to act as a handle, and cut a hole in the side of the castle wall slightly smaller than the portcullis. Demonstrate lifting the portcullis to let imaginary soldiers walk underneath, and then lower it again into place.

Finish the castle with flags made from fabric scraps and lolly sticks.

If this is to be a guided activity…

…then the children can work together in a small group of three or four children with an adult to create a box model castle. Support the children to create a castle with several features – stone effect walls, crenelated towers, turrets, drawbridge, portcullis etc. Use the appropriate vocabulary when designing and building, and encourage the children to do the same.

If this is to be an independent activity…

…then show the children where the box of resources will be, and explain that they can try this activity sometime this week. Let them work in small groups to build a castle, choosing roles for each other, for example the painter, the door maker, the drawbridge team. Encourage them to work together to add lots of features to their castles, decorating with flags and heraldry.

To support or extend

To support, help a child to build a castle-style building with the 3D wooden shapes. Use the correct names for the bricks. Support them by building alongside and then asking the child to imitate your structure – for example a cylinder with a cone on the top. Talk out loud whilst you are building, e.g. 'Now I'm going to build a wall for my castle – what could I use? These long straight bricks would make a good wall'. Take a photograph of the finished castle and show the child – which part do they like best? How would they alter it if they built it again?

To extend, let the children build a castle using the 3D wooden shapes. Photograph it (in case it falls down!) and give the children a sticky note pad. Ask them to label the key features of their castle and put the sticky notes on. Extend further by using the mathematical names for the shapes and counting how many of each there are. Create a simple table showing the frequency of each and talk through with the children what it shows.

Ideas for interactive display

- Display pictures and photographs of castles and large buildings from around the world. Attach clear labels of the castle parts (moat, turrets, walls, drawbridge) for the children to read and copy onto their drawings.

- Display a blueprint of a house or extension. Put out clipboards, pencils and flat shapes to draw around for the children to create their own plans of castles and buildings.

Parents and carers as partners

At home collect cardboard boxes, tubes, lids and packaging for your child to build with. Turn the boxes inside out so it is easier to draw or paint on them. Try to make a replica of something familiar to your child, like their home or a vehicle. Alternatively let your imagination run wild and create a fairy castle or a space rocket!

Castles and houses

Traditional homes from around the world

The children will be looking at castles, houses and homes from around the world, and building a collage of these on a large world map.

Observation and assessment

Understanding the world	Expected statements (ELGs)
People and communities	Children talk about past and present events in their own lives and the lives of family members. They know about similarities and differences between themselves and others, and among families, communities, and traditions.

Resources

- ★ Polystyrene chips, straw, fabric, sticks, pegs, paper, card and mud

- ★ Pictures and photographs of castles, houses and homes from around the world

- ★ Ice cubes

- ★ Marshmallows

- ★ Small bowls

- ★ Playdough

- ★ Large drapes, sheets, canes, poles and clothes pegs

Safety first!

Ensure that none of the children have allergies to any food being tasted.

Storybooks

- ★ *'Homes Around the World Series'* by Debbie Gallagher – includes *Palaces, Mansions and Castles; Portable Homes; River and Sea Homes; Mud, Grass and Ice Homes; City and Country Homes; Cave* and *Underground Homes.*

- ★ *Houses and Homes (Around the world series)* by Ann Morris

- ★ *Homes Around the World (Living in My World)* by Adam R Schaefer

- ★ *'Homes Around the World Series'* by Nicola Barber – includes *Island Homes; Mountain Home; Homes on the Move; Village Home; City Home; Waterside Home.*

Key vocabulary

- wall
- roof
- floor
- door
- shelter
- tipi
- igloo
- stilt bungalow
- thatched cottage
- house

What to do

Show the children the pictures and photographs of various buildings from around the world included in some of the books suggested above. Include buildings built for a particular purpose, e.g. nomad's homes which are easily portable, fishermen's stilt bungalows which are built out over water, igloos constructed from ice blocks and tipis constructed from poles and animal hides.

Explain that people in different parts of the world design and make their home according to their surrounding environment. Talk about the children's own homes and those around the local area – do they have sloping roofs? Explain that this is because the slopes help the frequent UK rain to run off into the gutters and drainpipes and down to the ground. Compare UK buildings with some pictures of Mediterranean or Greek homes (holiday brochures are useful for this). What is different about these houses? The flat roofs are suitable for the dry climate and the small windows keep the sun out.

Talk about the different materials from which buildings are made. Explain that castles were built to be strong and keep out enemies. This is why they are built from stone and have moats and drawbridges to prevent people from getting in. Discuss the different materials used to build homes in different places around the world and explain that people use materials they can find nearby. Show the children the selection of materials you have gathered together and explain that they are to build a model of a home.

If this is to be a guided activity…

…then the children can work together with an adult to build a home of their choice. Igloos are a good choice as they can be built authentically from ice cubes, built cleanly from polystyrene packaging chips or built stickily from marshmallows! Turn a small, shallow dish upside down and use this as a mould to put the 'bricks' around. When it is dry (use water as glue for the ice cubes or marshmallows) carefully separate the bowl from the igloo…and if it's marshmallow, eat it!

If this is to be an independent activity…

…then show the children where the materials are and explain that they can try this activity sometime this week. Include materials such as polystyrene chips, straw, fabric, sticks, pegs, paper, card and mud! Provide pictures of some different types of traditional home (tipi, igloo, stilt bungalow, thatched roof cottage etc.) for the children to refer to when making their version of a particular home. Provide the digital camera for the children to record their constructions.

To support or extend

To support, give the children some playdough to build with. Look at the pictures of different types of homes and let the children select one to copy. Help them to roll, shape and join the dough to make walls, roofs and floors. Use the appropriate vocabulary when building with the children and encourage them to closely observe the photographs of the homes from around the world in order to copy the key features.

To extend, challenge the children to design a home for a particular purpose or environment. Discuss the stilt bungalows, tree houses and nomad homes and talk about how they are suited to a particular purpose. Tell the children that they are to draw a design for a home for a river fisherman. Consider where he will need to live and work (on the river) and what type of a home he could have (a houseboat!)

Ideas for interactive display

- Display pictures and photographs of castles and large buildings from around the world. Put up a large map and join the pictures to their locations on the map with clear labels showing the name of the type of building and the name of the country.

- Outdoors, provide large drapes, sheets, canes, sticks, poles and clothes pegs for the children to make their own homes and shelters. Link these to the climbing frame or washing line so that the children can use the pre-existing structure.

Parents and carers as partners

At home, make homes and shelters indoors and out from sheets, blankets, canes, broom handles, laundry airers, washing lines, clothes pegs and tables. Children don't mind about the complexity or size of their den – a sheet simply draped over a table creating a hidey hole underneath is a fantastically exciting place for someone under five!

Castles and houses

Activity 4

Cereal castles

The children will be using mosaic paper squares and square breakfast cereal to build a crenelated castle on plain paper, adding towers, turrets and flags from fabric and paper.

Observation and assessment

Expressive arts and design	Expected statements (ELGs)
Exploring and using media and materials	They safely use and explore a variety of materials, tools and techniques, experimenting with colour, design, texture, form and function.
Being imaginative	Children use what they have learnt about media and materials in original ways, thinking about users and purposes. They represent their own ideas, thoughts and feelings through design and technology, art, music, dance, role-play and stories.

Key vocabulary

- collage
- brick
- flag
- square
- wall
- tower
- mosaic
- crenelated

Resources

- ★ Flipchart and paper
- ★ Small square breakfast cereal
- ★ Larger cereal rectangles
- ★ Biscuits and different shapes
- ★ Small cardboard squares
- ★ Cardboard background
- ★ Glue
- ★ Fabric
- ★ Coloured/patterned paper
- ★ Art straws
- ★ Skipping ropes, drapes, crates, hosepipes, guttering, canes and poles

Storybooks and film clips

- ★ *Over at the Castle* by Boni Ashburn
- ★ *Creepy Castle* by Colin and Jacqui Hawkins

What to do

Look together at some of the books suggested for the earlier castle activities, including non-fiction and story books. Ask the children to look carefully at the pictures of the different castles because they are going to make a collage of one using card, paper, fabric and breakfast cereal for bricks. On a flipchart draw a simple outline of a castle, talking about the different shapes needed and the patterns created by the bricks and walls. On a piece of paper laid on the floor, use the cardboard squares, breakfast cereal and biscuits to make a collage castle. Ask the children to suggest what to include next. Fill in any spaces with cardboard squares and shapes, e.g. conical turrets. When it is complete ask the children to help you look back through the books at the pictures to see if there are any extra features which could be added, e.g. spaces for windows, flags and flagpoles. Use the art straws and other collage scraps to add the final features. When they are happy with the design, glue it down.

Explain to the children that they are going to make a collage of their own castle and they can add as many towers, turrets, windows and walls as they like.

If this is to be a guided activity…

…then the children can work together in a group with an adult to create a small group collage of a castle. Talk together about what each child wants to include and look through the books together to find a picture which contains these elements. Use the picture as the design to copy, choosing appropriately sized and shaped cereal, biscuits and cardboard to add texture and different effects.

If this is to be an independent activity…

…then show the children where the box of art resources will be, and explain that they can try this activity sometime this week. Let the children make their collage castle shape dry, without gluing it down. Include larger cereal squares, rectangles and biscuits in different shapes for the children to arrange into castles, houses and mansions. Let one group of children follow another in order to create an entire street of buildings! Take photographs at each stage of building, as these dry collages are very fragile.

To support or extend

To support, take the children into a large space and as a group show them how to use their bodies to make different shapes. Begin initially by asking the children to lie down on the floor and make a straight shape, then a curved shape. Put the children into groups of four. Ask them to lie down together and make a long straight line with their bodies, then a circular shape. Some children might find this difficult. To make it easier, choose a group of children and help them make the shape first in order for the other children to copy. Depending upon the capability of the children, extend further to making triangles and square shapes, or simplify it by asking the children to lie along pre-drawn chalk lines or skipping ropes laid in a shape.

To extend, let the children use large props to make a giant castle. This activity works well outdoors. Use skipping ropes, drapes, crates, hosepipes, guttering, canes and poles to 'build' a collage of a castle or mansion on the ground. Work in a team to build different parts or features of the castle. Put a table or bench at the foot of the design so that the children can look at their design from a height in order to make any changes.

Ideas for interactive display

- Provide a quiet area for the children to look at the collection of castle books. Alongside this provide a selection of flat shapes and trays for the children to build castles upon.

- Put out squared paper for the children to colour in squares in a castle design. Provide some construction toys such as Lego, Sticklebricks or Mosaics for the children to further explore castle designs.

Parents and carers as partners

At home, make collages using objects from around the home. If the collage is kept dry and not glued down then many household objects can be borrowed for temporary use and returned afterwards. For example, make a collage picture of a crown using shiny cutlery, coins and jewellery; or a life-sized collage of a child using actual clothing and a paper plate for their face! Be creative, indoors and out!

Armour and battles

Coat of arms

The children will be making a personal coat of arms using initial letters in their name.

Resources

- ★ Pictures of coats of arms
- ★ Cards with letters of the alphabet on them
- ★ Card
- ★ Card stencils of shield shapes
- ★ Pre-cut card shield shapes
- ★ Crayons
- ★ Toy catalogues, character magazines
- ★ Glue
- ★ Scissors
- ★ Selection of personal objects linked to the adult leading the session (e.g. a football shirt, an instrument, a religious item, evidence of a hobby etc.)

Storybooks and non-fiction books

- ★ *How To Be a Knight* by David Steer
- ★ *Design Your Own Coat of Arms: Introduction to Heraldry* by Rosemary A. Chorzempa
- ★ *Coat of Arms* by Catherine Daly-Weir

Observation and assessment

Communication and Language	Expected statements (ELGs)
Listening and attention	Children listen attentively in a range of situations. They listen to stories, accurately anticipating key events and respond to what they hear with relevant comments, questions or actions.
Understanding	Children follow instructions involving several ideas or actions.

Literacy	Expected statements (ELGs)
Writing	Children use their phonic knowledge to write words in ways which match their spoken sounds. They also write some irregular common words. They write simple sentences which can be read by themselves and others. Some words are spelt correctly and others are phonetically plausible.

Key vocabulary

- alphabet
- letter
- name
- sound
- phoneme
- initial
- hobby
- belief
- significance
- represent

What to do

With the children seated around, begin to bring out the personal objects linked to the adult. With each object discuss with the children how it represents something that is important such as a hobby, a belief or family. Show the children some coats of arms with pictures and symbols on them.

Explain to the children that long ago people developed coats of arms as a means of identification or belonging. Look at one or two, encouraging the children to guess what the name or pastimes of the owner of the coat of arms might have been by looking at the pictures and symbols used. Show the children the pre-cut card shield shapes and explain that they are going to design their own coat of arms using the initial letters of their name and pictures showing things that interest or 'represent' them the most. Introduce the key vocabulary.

Play a little 'stand up/sit down' game using the initial letter cards. Ensure that each child knows which letter of the alphabet is at the beginning of their first name and explain that when the adult holds up a card the children with the same initial stand up. When a different letter is held up, they sit down again. This activity can be extended by holding up more than one card at a time or by using different letters, e.g. the initial letter in the surname, the phoneme (e.g. ch, sh, th), the name of the letter (e.g. E for Evie), the sound of the letter (e.g. E for Ella) or the letter itself (e.g. E for Ewan!).

Discuss with the children the type of drawing or picture they can add to their shield. Show them the toy catalogues and character magazines and explain that they can cut out pictures of things that show their hobby and favourite things such as a football, a bike or a character from television or film. Encourage each of the children to contribute, stating what they would choose to include.

If this is to be a guided activity…

…then the children can work together with an adult to create their own shield or coat of arms. Help them to draw their initial letter on first before decorating the shield with drawings and pictures cut from magazines. When finished, gather together the coats of arms and look at them together. Invite the children to try to guess who each one belongs to based upon the initial letter and pictures chosen, giving reasons for their choices.

If this is to be an independent activity…

…then show the children where the magazines, shield outlines and letter stencils are and explain that they are to create their own coat of arms sometime during the week. Have the book of ideas nearby for the children to look at. Talk to them about drawing pictures which also give clues to their identity. This is easier for some names than others, for example girls' names from flowers (Lily, Daisy, Poppy etc.) and some surnames can be recorded pictorially.

To support or extend

To support, have some shields pre-cut with different initial letters drawn on them. Working with a small group of around four children (ideally whose names begin with different initial letters) spread out the shields. Talk with the children about the alphabet, sing it through and ask the children to pick up the shield with their initial on when the song reaches it. Support the children to colour in their letter and decorate around the edge of their coat of arms with pictures of themselves and things they like to do.

To extend, make a shield for a famous person or character from a familiar story. For example, a footballer from a favourite team may have a coat of arms in distinctive team colours decorated with a football or boots. A character from a story book may have items featured in their stories or films. Display these together with pictures or photographs of the characters for the children to pair up.

Ideas for interactive display

Display a collection of coats of arms or shields in the classroom. Begin with items with which the children are familiar (the local school uniform, local travel companies and sportswear). Provide pencils and paper on the display so that the children can create a coat of arms for a person or group that they know well, such as their dance class or school football team. Put out drawing pins so that the children can attach these to the class display.

Parents and carers as partners

At home, look for coats of arms and shields in the local environment.
They are often found on vehicles, maps, signs, council documents, coins, company logos, school uniform and sportswear. Talk with the children about what the different aspects signify. Work together to create a family coat of arms showing the people in your family.

Armour and battles

Clothes peg catapult!

The children will be building a catapult from clothes pegs and a spoon, and measuring the distance an object is flung.

Resources

★ Pictures of castle and trebuchet

★ Lolly sticks or a scrap of flat wood approximately 10 cm x 10 cm

★ Wooden clothes pegs

★ Glue (PVA or glue gun)

★ Plastic spoon or plastic milk bottle lid

★ Cotton wool balls

★ Pom-pom balls

★ Ping pong ball

★ Marble

★ Other missiles (e.g. pen lids, small coins, gravel etc.)

★ Beanbags

★ Hoops or buckets

★ Tiddlywinks in different colours

Storybooks and non-fiction books

★ *Siege (Knights and Castles)* by Laura Durman

★ *Little Book of Castles (Usbourne Little Books)* by Lesley Sims

Observation and assessment

Mathematics	Expected statements (ELGs)
Number	Children count reliably with numbers from 1 to 20, place them in order and say which number is one more or one less than a given number.
Shape, space and measures	Children use everyday language to talk about size, weight, capacity, position, distance, time and money to compare quantities and objects and to solve problems. They explore characteristics of everyday objects and shapes and use mathematical language to describe them.

Key vocabulary

- catapult
- trebuchet
- defence
- enemies
- protect
- flick
- missile

What to do

Talk with the children about how castles were important buildings and that their role was to defend against enemies. Look at a picture of a castle and discuss the purpose of the moat, the drawbridge, the narrow slit windows and the battlements. Explain that because initially they were built a long time ago there were limited means of attack and defence; namely arrows, boiling water/tar, battering rams and catapults. Introduce and reinforce the key vocabulary. If you have a model of a castle (either a small world toy or something built by the children in an earlier activity) use toys to simulate attacking the castle. Demonstrate how the moat and the high walls made it extremely difficult to enter the castle and take control. Introduce the idea of a catapult (or trebuchet) designed to fire a missile at the walls, or indeed over the walls into the castle. Use a ruler to show the children how something could be flicked up and over and into the castle. Explain that they are going to build a catapult together and investigate what missiles are most successfully fired.

Put the flat piece of wood on the table (if you don't have one you could tape ten lolly sticks together laid flat side by side). Glue on the wooden clothes peg so that if you press down on the top it opens the pinching end. This pressing motion is to be the lever end. Glue a spoon onto the part of the clothes peg you pressed with your finger (but leave a little peg sticking out the end for your finger to press down upon). If you don't have a spoon, glue a lolly stick onto the top of the peg and then glue the upturned lid almost at the end of the stick. Put a cotton wool ball, pom-pom or something else light and similar into the spoon or lid. Press down on the end of the clothes peg with your finger to open it, and let go! The object in the spoon or lid will fly into the air!

If this is to be a guided activity…

…then the children can work together in a small group with an adult to build a catapult. Investigate firing different objects into the air, considering weight, size and dimensions before loading it up. Encourage the children to make predictions before firing the missile, considering weight, height, distance travelled and direction. If it is possible fire into an actual toy castle, awarding points for missiles launched over the castle walls.

If this is to be an independent activity…

…then show the children where the box of resources will be, and explain that they can use any of the materials provided to build a catapult-style device. Include stiff card, bendy plastic rulers, cutlery, clothes pegs and various different construction sets. Tell the children that the only rule is that their device must flick a simple missile into the air, e.g. a cotton wool ball. Demonstrate the simplest idea (holding a cotton wool ball against a bent back ruler, and releasing the sprung end) showing how the cotton wool ball is moved forwards. Gather together at the end of the session to consider different design ideas.

Armour and battles

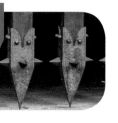

Moving armour

The children will be making some moving armour (a headband with visor) using cardboard, foil and split pins.

Observation and assessment

Understanding the world	Expected statements (ELGs)
The world	Children know about similarities and differences in relation to places, objects, materials and living things.
Technology	Children recognise that a range of technology is used in places such as homes and schools. They select and use technology for particular purposes.

Resources

★ Picture of a knight wearing armour

★ Split pins

★ Stapler

★ Paper plates

★ Scissors

★ Card

★ Foil

★ Sticky tape

★ Glue stick

★ Black wax crayon

Storybooks and non-fiction books

★ *Small Knight and George* by Rhonda Armitage

★ *Arms and Armour (Eyewitness)* by Michelle Byam

Key vocabulary

• armour	• split pin	• cut
• visor	• pivot	• shape
• helmet	• join	• move

What to do

Look at the picture of the knight wearing armour. Talk about each part of the amour in turn, encouraging the children to point to the part of their body it would cover and why it would need protection. Discuss why some parts of the armour would need to move – how could the knight eat if the helmet did not separate from the body of the armour? Introduce the key vocabulary. Explain that the eye and upper face protection is called a visor. Remind the children that some people wear these today for their jobs, e.g. a fireman, scientist or metalworker. Tell the children that they are going to make a simple headband and attach a moving visor to look like a piece of armour.

Make a band to fit around a child's head from cardboard. If this is wrapped in silver foil it will look like shiny metal. Cut a paper plate in half and wrap both halves in foil. Using a glue stick on the plate first will ensure the foil stays in place. These will separately become the upper and lower half of the visor. Both can move if attached with split pins. To make it simpler attach one half of the plate securely (the lower half) to the band with staples. When the child puts on the band like a crown the lower paper plate will sit in front of their nose and mouth. Cut strips from the long straight side of the other half of paper plate to make a 'grille' effect that the children can see through. Join this 'grille' paper plate to the band with split pins so that it moves up and down protecting the eyes.

If this is to be a guided activity…

…then the children can work together with an adult to make a helmet with a moving visor. The adult will need to help in measuring the head band, stapling the band and the lower nose and mouth protection and joining using the split pins. The children can decorate with silver foil and draw with black wax crayon to add detail to their helmet and visor.

If this is to be an independent activity…

…then show the children where the pre-cut paper plates, head bands and foil are and explain that they are to investigate joining the visor to the band with the split pins. If the children are unfamiliar with split pins then demonstrate how to use them by pressing the point into the card over a ball of Plasticine to avoid injuries. A paper plate could be pre-cut into the grille shape for the children to use as a stencil and draw around before cutting independently.

Glue Stick

To support or extend

To support, make a helmet using only a band around the head and a single half paper plate attached with split pins to the band. This will move up and down to protect the eyes in a manner similar to protective face masks worn by metalworkers or gardeners strimming grass! Help the children to cut out strips from the visor by holding the half plate for them so they simply have to cut along the lines drawn on the plate.

To extend, provide card, foil, sticky tape and split pins for the children to use to develop their own armour. Using the pictures of knights wearing armour encourage the children to think about which other parts of the body may need protection and allow them to design and make their own. Talk about why it is necessary and how it will function.

Ideas for interactive display

Put out different types of construction toys on the display table and invite the children to make protective headgear from it. Display these alongside a collection of other types of protective clothing including safety helmets, glasses, riding hats, cycle helmets and protective sportswear. Display photographs of sporting heroes wearing protective clothing (helmets, shin pads, mouth guards etc) and highlight their necessity.

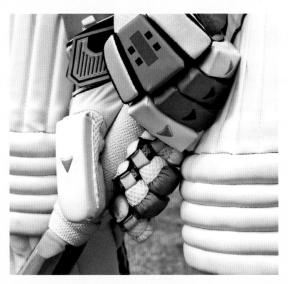

Parents and carers as partners

At home look out for other examples of protective clothing that keeps us safe. Talk with your child about the importance of wearing a helmet when cycling, skating, horse riding, using a scooter or roller skating. Look through a catalogue which has more protective clothing such as knee pads or elbow pads. There may be someone in the family who needs protective clothing for their work – talk together about what it is and what job it does.

Armour and battles

Life-sized knight collage

The children will be using shiny collage to make a life-sized knight in armour.

Resources

- ★ Pictures of armour worn by medieval knights
- ★ Simple outline of a knight in armour on A4 paper
- ★ Roll of lining paper/large piece of cardboard
- ★ Shiny collage materials
- ★ Foil
- ★ Silver coloured pan scourers
- ★ Silver tinsel and glitter
- ★ Silver metallic card
- ★ Silver foil effect sticky tape/silver duct tape
- ★ Glue
- ★ Scissors
- ★ Sticky tape
- ★ Silver paint
- ★ Silver crayons
- ★ Collection of silver items, e.g. pans, pan lids, metal sieves, colanders, cutlery
- ★ Pictures of sculptures by Giacometti

Storybooks

- ★ *King Arthur and the Knights of the Round Table* (Illustrated Classics) by Marcia Williams
- ★ *Armour* (Usbourne Beginners) by Catriona Clarke

Observation and assessment

Expressive arts and design	Expected statements (ELGs)
Exploring and using media and materials	They safely use and explore a variety of materials, tools and techniques, experimenting with colour, design, texture, form and function.
Being imaginative	Children use what they have learnt about media and materials in original ways, thinking about uses and purposes.

Key vocabulary

- armour
- helmet
- breastplate
- gauntlets
- visor
- sabatons
- metal
- chainmail
- lance

What to do

Explain to the children that they are going to work as a team to create a child-sized collage of a knight. Choose a child to lie down on the lining paper/cardboard and draw around them to create the initial outline. Look at pictures of knights wearing armour in the books and discuss together the main pieces required. Highlight particularly the helmet, visor, breastplate, gauntlets (gloves) and sabatons (feet and lower leg protectors). Introduce the key vocabulary, helping the children to use it correctly when they are talking. Look at the selection of collage materials available – help the children to select the most appropriate material for the purpose, giving justification for their reasons. For example, the silver duct tape might make effective gauntlets as it could be cut into strips and layered on around each hand; or the silver coloured pan scourers may make effective shoulder epaulettes.

If this is to be a guided activity…

…then the children can work together in a group with an adult to draw around one child to create a child-sized knight. Encourage each child to make a contribution, working as a team to select and apply each collage material. Support the children in justifying their choices, and demonstrate simple reasoning, speaking and listening. When complete, cut out the knight and display him 'standing' on the floor against a display wall. Print the background using a brick shaped sponge and grey paint to create castle walls. Line up a collection of knights in armour together – they do not all have to be standing with their arms at their sides – create some battle poses!

If this is to be an independent activity…

…then show the children where the box of art resources will be, and explain that they can try this activity sometime this week. Provide the silver collage materials on a much smaller scale (e.g. small mosaic squares of silver foil) along with an outline on A4 paper of a knight wearing armour. Talk with the children about how in a collage the different textures and finishes are suitable for different parts of the artwork or picture. Encourage them to colour some sections with silver wax crayons to give a flat texture, and to contrast this with glued mosaic foil squares for a shiny texture and silver glitter for a sparkly texture. Encourage them to consider symmetry when collaging (e.g. both gauntlets to have the same finish).

To support or extend

To support, have a collection of large items made from metal or shiny silver coloured plastic for the children to use to make a large-scale design. For example, use kitchen items such as pans and lids, metal colanders and sieves, ladles, cutlery, metal trays and baking equipment to 'build' a picture. A knight may be too challenging here, but an alien, robot or vehicle can be added to and imagined. Simply lay the items on the ground creating a picture, reminding the children to choose objects according to size and effect; for example to look like wheels, doors, or eyes for a robot.

To extend, give the children some silver foil and let them practise rolling, scrunching and pressing the foil to model with it. Beginning with a small thin cylinder type shape (body) twist and scrunch more foil sausages to add arms and legs. Look at some pictures of sculptures by Giacometti for inspiration. Display these pictures alongside the finished models.

Ideas for interactive display

- Provide an area of shiny silver coloured collage bits and pieces for the children to use to create their own silver collage pictures. These look great displayed on black paper or card.

- On the wall put a large clear picture of a knight in armour. Attach card labels (helmet, visor, breastplate, gauntlets, sabatons) to long pieces of string and hang them on the wall all together. Using Blu tack or adhesive Velcro buttons invite the children to put the correct label on the correct part of the armour. When complete, photograph their efforts, pull the labels free again so they hang on their string and invite someone else to try.

Parents and carers as partners

At home, collect shiny things to make a collage picture with. Include foil, wrappers, lids, screws, nuts, bolts, coins and cutlery. The collage doesn't have to be glued down (you'll probably need the cutlery for dinnertime!) but simply placed on a tray in a design. Sweep it all off into a box and make the picture again tomorrow.

Dangerous dragons!

Dragon design

The children will be drawing and labelling a dragon of their own design, explaining their chosen features.

Key vocabulary

- scales
- teeth
- claws
- talons
- tail
- spines
- fire
- wings
- nostrils

Resources

- ★ Pictures of dragons
- ★ Photographs of chameleons, iguanas and komodo dragons
- ★ Playdough
- ★ Flipchart
- ★ Paper
- ★ Pencils and crayons
- ★ Sticky notes
- ★ Glue

Storybooks and non-fiction books

- ★ *Tell Me a Dragon* by Jackie Morris
- ★ *Too Hot to Hug* by Steve Smallman
- ★ *That's Not my Dragon!* by Fiona Watt

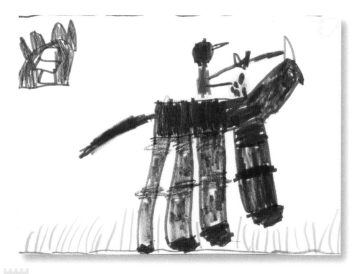

Observation and assessment

Communication and Language	Expected statements (ELGs)
Understanding	They answer 'how' and 'why' questions about their experiences and in response to stories or events.

Literacy	Expected statements (ELGs)
Writing	Children use their phonic knowledge to write words in ways which match their spoken sounds. They also write some irregular common words. They write simple sentences which can be read by themselves and others. Some words are spelt correctly and others are phonetically plausible.

What to do

Read some dragon storybooks and look at the pictures together. What do all the dragons have in common? Make a list of features on the flipchart, using clear labels including tail, scales, talons or claws, nostrils, spines and wings when introducing the key vocabulary. Explain to the children that dragons are imaginary animals that do not exist in life but that there are lots of stories and legends about them. Show the photographs of reptiles which are thought to look like dragons, and draw parallels with the labels of dragon parts they listed on the flipchart. Discuss why these reptiles need these features, for example they have claws to catch and eat prey; tails to help move, climb and balance. Ensure that the children recognise that there are some aspects of fictional dragons that are not found in reptiles, such as fire-breathing, flying and smoking nostrils!

Show a large, clear picture of a dragon to the children. Encourage a child to identify one aspect of the dragon (e.g. wings) and to say why they are needed (e.g. to fly to the top of a mountain where it lives). Write this onto sticky notes or card labels and attach to the picture near to the relevant body part. Repeat this with other children and other parts of the dragon.

If this is to be a guided activity…

…then the children can work together with an adult to design an imaginary dragon of their own. Look at the features identified in the group activity and decide which of these to include on their own design. Explain that as dragons are not actual creatures then they can have as many legs, wings or spines as can be imagined! Encourage the children to write labels justifying the selection of each feature, or adult to act as scribe.

If this is to be an independent activity…

…then show the children where the paper, pencils, dragon storybooks and reptile non-fiction books are and explain that they are to draw a dragon of their own design, including the main features of the dragons in the stories. If they want to add other features they can, labelling and explaining their choices to an adult.

To support or extend

To support, use photographs of actual reptiles for the children to cut up and collage together to design a dragon of their own. Talk about what they may need ('a long spiky tail') and look through some photographs of reptiles to choose one suitable. Glue onto a piece of paper and add further features. Finish by giving their imaginary dragon a name.

To extend, use playdough to make a model of a dragon with the key features listed on the flipchart. Show the children how to pinch, press, tweak, twist and pull the dough to make spines, scales and claws without using any tools, just their hands. Display them all together in a group. When they are dry they may be painted.

Ideas for interactive display

Divide a display board in half. On one side display pictures, photographs and models of reptiles which exist in the world. Label their features with keywords and simple facts. On the other half of the board display pictures of dragons, along with the dragon designs the children have produced. On the table put out a selection of dragon storybooks and simple non-fiction books about reptiles. Ensure that the children understand that dragons are legendary and not real.

Parents and carers as partners

At home draw pictures of different animals, or cut pictures of them from magazines. Group similar animals together – these all live in water, these all have feathers, these all have horns. Talk together about how the animals have been grouped and why.

Dangerous dragons!

Dice dragons

The children will be building a dragon by rolling dice and adding numbered body parts.

Resources

★ Dice (one numbered 1–6 another 7–12)

★ Simple dragon picture – laminated

★ Four copies of the same dragon picture cut into body parts

★ Sticky labels

Storybooks and non-fiction books

★ *The Egg* by M. P. Robertson

★ *The Great Dragon Rescue* by M. P. Robertson

Observation and assessment

Mathematics	Expected statements (ELGs for end of F2)
Number	Children count reliably with numbers from 1 to 20, place them in order and say which number is one more or one less than a given number. Using quantities and objects, they add and subtract two single-digit numbers and count on or back to find the answer.

Key vocabulary

body	head	five
legs	one	six
wings	two	dice
tail	three	
spines	four	

What to do

Look at a picture of a dragon together and name the main body parts including head, body, tail, legs, spines and wings. Show the children the laminated picture of the dragon and explain that each part is to have a number. Put stickers on the dragon as follows: 1 – body, 2 – head, 3 – tail, 4 – spines, 5 – wing(s), 6 – leg(s). Write matching numbers on the body parts already cut up. Demonstrate how to play the game to the children. Roll a large dice so that the children can see the spots and count them and say what number it is. Match the number of spots on the dice to the numerals on the dragon body parts, selecting the matching one as the first piece of your dragon. Let a child take a turn to roll a dice and select the matching numbered dragon part. If you roll a number you already have then play moves on to the next person. The winner is the first person to build a complete dragon.

If this is to be a guided activity…

…then the children can work together in a small group with an adult to make and play the game. Give each of them a dragon picture and six sticky numbers and talk them through the body parts, naming them with the correct vocabulary. Help them to cut them up and spread them out on the table altogether. Take turns to roll the dice and select a matching numbered piece from the table. The first child to build a complete dragon is the winner.

If this is to be an independent activity…

…then show the children where the box of resources will be, and explain that they can try this activity sometime this week. Let them work in small groups to play the game and match the pieces together. If your children are able to work with larger numbers exchange the 1–6 dice for the 7–12 dice. Provide whiteboards and pens so the children can record the frequency of rolling a particular number as an example of emergent mathematics.

To support, simplify the animal picture to have fewer parts, or use only numbers which the children recognise. Count the spots on the dice with them and match to the appropriate number. To make it even simpler arrange the numbered body parts in order in a line in front of each child so that they can count by rote, pointing to each card as they say the number name.

To extend, let the children draw and design their own creature to make into a dice game. Explain that it needs to have body parts that can be numbered and put together like a jigsaw – it is no use drawing a slug! Photocopy their original drawing so that the game parts are identical to the original and allow the children to play each others' games to test them out.

Ideas for interactive display

Provide a selection of different number games for the children to play together. Let them select their own counters, rules and criteria for winning, for example throwing a six means go first; throwing a six means have another turn; play stops when the first child wins; play stops when the last child finishes. Provide whiteboards for the children to record their game rules by drawing and emergent writing.

Parents and carers as partners

At home make a simple game of your own. Cut up two identical pictures of animals or characters from the television and write numbers 1 to 6 on each part. Take turns to roll the dice, count the spots and match the number on the body part – the winner is the first to collect an entire animal!

Dangerous dragons!

Dragon: WANTED!

The children will be talking about which jobs would be suitable for a dragon and writing a job advert.

Observation and assessment

Understanding the world	Expected statements (ELGs)
People	They know about similarities and differences between themselves and others, and among families, communities and traditions.
The world	Children know about similarities and differences in relation to places, objects, materials and living things. They make observations of animals and plants and explain why some things occur, and talk about changes.

Key vocabulary

- breathing fire
- spines
- talons
- job advertisement
- characteristic

Resources

- Flipchart
- Whiteboards
- Paper
- Pencils

Storybooks and non-fiction books

- *The Dragon who Couldn't Help Breathing Fire* by Denis Bond
- *The Trouble with Dragons* by Debi Gliori
- *The Dragon who Couldn't Do Dragony Things* by Anni Axworthy

What to do

Read some of the dragon books to the children. Talk together about some of the problems the dragons in the stories encountered linked to breathing fire or having spiky spines, a long tail and sharp talons etc. Explain to the children that although we are all people we all look different and all of us are good at different things. Discuss with the children the things that they are good at and the things they are not so good at, drawing their attention to the fact that different children within the group give different answers. Choose a common problem suffered by the dragon, e.g. breathing fire. Talk about why this is dangerous and what would happen if a dragon came in to the setting and tried to teach the children – things would catch on fire! But can the children think of a job that needs fire which the dragon would be very suited to? (For example lighting fires on Bonfire Night or being the flame burner in a space rocket). Choose another seemingly negative characteristic of the dragon which could be turned into a positive: spiky spines could help dry washing; a long scaly tail could make a super bat in a sports game! Let the children be as imaginative as possible, they will think of ideas that you will not! Discuss how people obtain jobs – employers who are looking for someone with a particular characteristic put up an advertisement for people to read. Explain to the children that they are going to make an advertisement for a role that a dragon would be suited to.

If this is to be a guided activity…

…then the children can work together with an adult to create a job advert. In a small group decide together what characteristic of the dragon will be needed in the job. When these have been decided, take turns to each suggest a useful purpose to this characteristic with the adult acting as scribe on the flipchart. The children can record all of these ideas on a piece of paper under the heading WANTED! either by drawing sketches or writing simple labels and captions, with support.

If this is to be an independent activity…

…then show the children where the paper and pencils are and explain that they can try this activity sometime this week. Provide simple writing frames to encourage the children to record their ideas through drawing, labels and simple caption sentences. Make a word bank using pictures and matching words to enable the children to find words independently, e.g. fire, tail, candles, dragon etc. Display these together on the interactive display to give the other children more ideas.

To support or extend

To support, think of a job where breathing fire would be useful. Together with an adult working as scribe record the ideas on a poster together, headed, 'Can you?…' The children can draw the fire breathing dragon performing its useful roles (e.g. lighting birthday candles, baking bread) and the adult can add labels suggested by the children. The finished item will be a poster advertising for someone (or something) who can breathe fire.

To extend, think of animals which would be suited to particular roles because of their physical characteristics, e.g. an elephant to wash cars by squirting water through its trunk or a giraffe to look for fruit growing high in a tree. Draw a picture of the animal performing the particular role and annotate around the edge with labels and captions.

Ideas for interactive display

Display pictures of different animals in a line on the wall. Underneath provide a few pictures of people dressed in clothing specific to a role, for example a diver, a pilot, a workman digging holes in the ground. The animal photographs should be those which may be linked to that role, e.g. a frog, a bird and a mole! Show the children how to link the pictures together by placing the animal picture alongside the corresponding person.

Parents and carers as partners

At home play role-play games with your child based upon people who help us in the community. Include roles familiar to the children such as shopkeepers, postmen and bus drivers. Set up a simple scene at home (a row of cushions for a bus, a collection of items to buy in the 'shop', a pile of letters in a bag to be 'delivered' around the room) and use props such as a hat or an apron to distinguish the roles. Talk about what the people do and why it is important.

Dangerous dragons!

Dragon's tail board game

The children will be making a board game based upon snakes and ladders; climbing up Rapunzel's hair and sliding down a dragon's tail.

Observation and assessment

Expressive arts and design	Expected statements (ELGs)
Exploring and using media and materials	They safely use and explore a variety of materials, tools and techniques, experimenting with colour, design, texture, form and function.
Being imaginative	Children use what they have learnt about media and materials in original ways, thinking about uses and purposes. They represent their own ideas, thoughts and feelings through design and technology, art, music, dance, role-play and stories.

Resources

* Examples of snakes and ladders board game – different versions if possible
* Large 100 square to step on
* 25 (5 x 5) squares photocopied in black and white
* 25 carpet tiles
* Yellow or gold rope
* Green pieces of fabric
* Dice
* Counters of different colours
* Squared paper
* Yellow ribbon
* Green felt cut into narrow triangles
* Unifix
* Chalk
* Crayons

Storybooks and non-fiction books

* *George, the Dragon and the Princess* by Christopher Wormell
* *George and the Dragon* by Christopher Wormell

Key vocabulary

* board game
* snakes and ladders
* climb up
* slide down
* more
* less
* forwards
* backwards
* count

What to do

Ask the children if anyone has played snakes and ladders, and encourage them to try to explain it to the other children. What is it? How is it set out? How do you play it? What do you need? Explain to the children that you are going to look at the board game snakes and ladders together and make a version of their own using dragons and Rapunzel! Begin with the carpet tiles, laying them out in a 5 x 5 square. If they are not numbered already, number them with chalk from 1 to 25 in the manner of a board game, where the numbers lead along from 1 to 5 then double back upon themselves from 6 to 10 and so on. Ask a child to step on each carpet tile as the rest of the children count out loud. Do this forward and backwards until the children are secure at counting in sequence by rote. Using the key vocabulary introduce the idea of Rapunzel's hair helping the player to 'climb up' to the next row of numbers. Place several pieces of yellow rope on the squares to join up the different rows. Roll a dice and choose two children to move along in the manner of counters. If they stand on a square with the bottom of a yellow rope on it they can climb to the next row. The winner is the person who reaches the top first. Remind the children that in snakes and ladders people don't just climb up, they also slide down snakes. Explain that in this game the snakes have been replaced by dragons' tails, represented by the green fabric. Place several pieces of green fabric on the grid connecting some rows, and play the game again this time sliding down the dragons' tails too.

If this is to be a guided activity...

...then the children can work together in a group with an adult to create their own version of snakes and ladders on paper, using Rapunzel's hair and dragons' tails. Give them a square containing a grid of numbers appropriate for their ability, e.g. 20, 25 or 50 squares. Firstly help them to number each square in the manner of a sequential board game, not a traditional 100 square. Following this give them several pieces of yellow ribbon to represent Rapunzel's hair and some narrow green felt triangles to represent the dragons' tail. Show them how to place them onto their game board and cut them to size until they are content with their position, finally gluing them down. Finish by playing the game with a friend.

If this is to be an independent activity...

...then show the children where the box of art resources will be, and explain that they can try this activity sometime this week. Put out numbered carpet tiles or laminated numbers on A4 card for the children to place on the floor as an array. Vary the amount of tiles according to the ability of the children. Provide yellow rope and green fabric of different lengths for the children to use to represent Rapunzel's hair for climbing or dragons' tails for sliding down. Put out squared paper and crayons so that the children can record the game board that they created in real life. The digital camera will also be useful in storing the image of their game. These images and drawings can be laminated and used as plans for other children to follow and recreate.

To support or extend

To support, go outdoors with chalk and create a simple number track upon the ground. Take it in turns to throw a dice and jump along the line in turn. Who will get to the end of the line first? To extend the game throw two differently coloured dice – move forwards according to the number on one and backwards according to the number on the other. Will they ever get to the end?

To extend, use larger amounts of squares (up to 50, 75, 100) for the children to create their board game. Provide small number tiles or Unifix for the children to firstly investigate suitable arrays. Following this provide them with squared paper so they can copy their array onto paper and write numbers in order in each square. Decorate with pictures and play the game with a friend.

Ideas for interactive display

Provide an area outdoors where the children can lay out the carpet tiles and make their own game. Provide props from the classroom (dice, counters, toy animals, bricks, construction etc.) and let the children experiment by laying out the numbered squares in different formations for different games. If possible, give the children some chalk for drawing on the ground so that they can draw their own board games and invent different types of games.

Parents and carers as partners

At home play simple board games together such as snakes and ladders and Ludo. This will help your child to learn valuable social skills ready for school such as turn taking, sharing and talking in a pair or small group. Other games such as Snap, Dominoes, I spy and Hopscotch all help with listening, counting, numbers and letter sounds.

Knight journeys

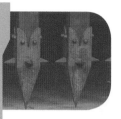

A knight's walk

The children will be retelling Rosie's Walk as the journey of a knight, using positional language including over, under, around, past and through.

Resources

- ★ Toy knight
- ★ Flipchart
- ★ Large pieces of paper
- ★ Pencil crayons
- ★ Small world buildings and scenery
- ★ Word cards with positional and directional language
- ★ Lucky dip bag
- ★ Voice recorder
- ★ Large apparatus

Storybooks

- ★ *Rosie's Walk* by Pat Hutchins

Key vocabulary

• journey	• over	• past
• position	• under	• through
• distance	• around	

Observation and assessment

Communication and Language	Expected statements (ELGs)
Listening and attention	They listen to stories, accurately anticipating key events and respond to what they hear with relevant comments, questions or actions.
Understanding	Children follow instructions involving several ideas or actions.
Speaking	Children express themselves effectively, showing awareness of listeners' needs. They use past, present and future forms accurately when talking about events that have happened or are to happen in the future. They develop their own narratives and explanations by connecting ideas or events

Literacy	Expected statements (ELGs)
Reading	Children read and understand simple sentences.

What to do

Read *Rosie's Walk* together. Look at all the places that the hen walks and ensure that the children understand the positional and directional vocabulary that is used. Explain to the children that they are going to verbally make up their own story about a knight that goes for a walk and all the things that happen to him on his journey. Show the children the toy knight and ask them to imagine that he is going on a walk from the castle. Ask the children what he will walk past and what he will see on his journey. Write their answers onto the flipchart in a list for them to look at later. Discuss the story language in the book: 'Rosie the hen went for a walk'. Ask the children how this could be changed to tell the tale of the knight – does he need a name? What would be appropriate? Select a word of something he encounters from the list generated on the flipchart, for example a pond. Which word would describe how he passed it: over, under, through or around? Write their chosen word on the board at the side of the word 'pond'. Continue in the same way until all of the positional and directional words have been used. Show the children the small world objects and explain that they are to build a landscape for the toy knight, and as the adult moves the toy around the setting the children are to say the positional/directional word and the name of the object, e.g. 'over the pond'. Tell the narrative together, recording if possible for the children to listen to afterwards. Encourage all children to participate.

If this is to be a guided activity…

…then the children can work together with an adult to create a landscape using the small world objects for the toy knight to travel through. Working in a small group, give each child an object and let them decide which positional or directional word they are going to use to describe the knight's journey in relation to the obstacle. Put the objects together in a journey map and encourage the children to take turns in telling part of the narrative each.

If this is to be an independent activity…

…then show the children where the collection of small world objects and the toy knight is and explain that they will have the opportunity to try this activity sometime during the week. Let them use the small world items to build a landscape for the knight to travel through. Encourage them to use the positional and directional language in their retelling of the journey. Provide them with a voice recorder to enable them to record their narrative to listen to afterwards.

To support, use large apparatus in a space along with lucky dip word cards with positional and directional language written on. Select a card (e.g. over) and ask the children to climb over something in the room, this may be a bench, a mat, a ladder or a net on the floor. Repeat for other words including under, around, past and through. Finish off with the adult telling the narrative which the children can act out, building a sequence of movements.

To extend, have a lucky dip bag containing word cards with the positional and directional words on. Let the children choose a card, read the word and then choose an appropriate object from the small world collection to pair with the word. For example, if they chose the word 'under' then they could choose a bridge or a tree; the word 'through' might pair well with a pond or a building. Take turns to select a card and an object and set them out in a journey, then use the toy knight to tell the narrative for each part.

Ideas for interactive display

Display lots of small world animals, buildings and scenery along with a toy knight for the children to play with. Add some large sheets of paper or a roll of lining paper for the children to record their journey upon.

Parents and carers as partners

At home, use a favourite toy and set up an adventurous journey for them on the floor. Using everyday objects create obstacles such as buildings, bridges, water, dangerous animals and mountains for the toy to go around, past, over, under and through. Talk through the story whilst moving the toy along. If you have room, recreate this journey on a bigger scale for your child using blankets, cushions, chairs and a lot of imagination!

Knight journeys

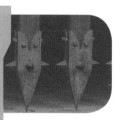

Roads and mazes

The children will be looking at roads, including direction, length, straight, curved and routes through mazes.

Observation and assessment

Mathematics	Expected statements (ELGs)
Shape, space and measures	Children use everyday language to talk about size, weight, capacity, position, distance, time and money to compare quantities and objects and to solve problems. They recognise, create and describe patterns.

Key vocabulary

- road
- path
- railway
- straight
- curved
- forward
- backwards
- long
- short
- maze

Resources

★ Photographs of mazes

★ Pencil mazes on paper

★ Railway track and roadway construction

★ Long ropes and canes

★ Chalk

★ Word cards with the key vocabulary on

★ Clipboards and paper

★ Aerial photographs of roads (straight and curved, including spaghetti junction)

Storybooks and non-fiction books

★ *Tales from Percy's Park – The Secret Path* by Nick Butterworth

★ *Dragon Mazes* by Roger Moreau

What to do

Read *The Secret Path* by Nick Butterworth. Talk to the children about paths and mazes – who has walked on a path today? Was it straight or curved? What was the difference? Discuss what a maze is; the children may have played in one before. Show the children the aerial photographs of roads and mazes and try travelling along one with your finger. Introduce and use the key vocabulary whilst you are showing the route. Explain to the children that they are going to build a maze of their own and that they are going to decide upon the directions needed to guide someone through it. Make a very simple 'L' shaped route on the floor using canes to mark the sides. Stand at the end of it and ask one of the children to tell you whether to move forward, backwards or sideways. When they say 'forwards' walk much too far and over the end of the 'L'. The children will shout with laughter, and you can use this as an example of the importance of indicating the distance for example, walk forwards two steps. Repeat until the children are able to guide you and others safely through the route. This can be extended in a place with markings on the floor, for example a tennis court or playground. Let the children work in pairs guiding each other with verbal instructions.

If this is to be a guided activity…

…then the children can work together in a small group with an adult to create a maze big enough for a child to pass through. Using chalk or rope and canes, mark on the ground a route for a child to follow. Ask them to close their eyes and then give them clear verbal instructions to help them negotiate the route. For example, ask them to take three steps forwards, turn to the right, take one small step etc. Let the children work together to guide each other through the maze, using the key vocabulary accurately.

If this is to be an independent activity…

…then show the children where the resources will be, and explain that they can try this activity sometime this week. Let them work in small groups to create a maze from rope and canes and then take it in turns to walk through it. Using a clipboard, ask them to note down in a list the instructions needed to travel through the route, for example forwards two steps, sideways one step, forwards four little steps. Use the laminated key vocabulary cards to help with the use of the mathematical language.

To support or extend

To support, put out the train track or roadway for the children to build with. Try to ensure that they build paths that have bridges or crossings so that the vehicles can travel around, over and under. Support the children when they are playing in using the key vocabulary by questioning, echoing and reinforcing their use and understanding of the words.

To extend, give the children an investigation using the train track or roadway. Limiting them to a certain number of pieces of straight and curved track, challenge them to make a particular shape. Can they make an oval? What is the longest straight run they can make if the track has to join at both ends? What other pieces will they need? Give them a digital camera to photograph their efforts and print out for other children to copy.

Ideas for interactive display

- Put out a thin layer of dry sand in a tray for the children to draw a track or a maze in with their finger. Place a black bin liner in the bottom to make the track easier to see. This can also be done using paint on a bin liner (and it's much more fun!) but could be messy on a display.

- Provide lots of example of mazes for children to investigate. As well as the small tilting ones containing a ball bearing there are 3D dimensional ones made from wood or metal which provide puzzles for people to solve.

Parents and carers as partners

At home use chalk to draw a crazy maze on the ground. Let your child take the chalk on a walk around and around, crossing over itself and creating a pathway for a car to follow. Use objects to add interest to your crazy maze such as grass, stones, toys and other chalked pictures in order to tell a story about what the car passes on its journey.

Knight journeys

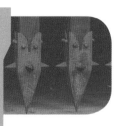

Follow the journey

The children will be creating a map showing the route of 'the kiss that missed' in a story.

Observation and assessment

Understanding the world	Expected statements (ELGs)
The world	Children know about similarities and differences in relation to places, objects, materials and living things. They talk about the features of their own immediate environment and how environments might vary from one another.

Key vocabulary

- miss
- float
- journey
- wild wood
- dragon
- wolves
- owls
- bears
- squirrels
- birds

Resources

★ Toy dragon, wolves, owls and bears

★ Pictures of wolves, owls and bears

★ Pictures of creatures that might live in a wood (birds, squirrels, dormice and snakes)

★ Paper

★ Pencils

★ Silver crayon or pen

Storybooks and non-fiction books

★ *The Kiss That Missed* by David Melling

★ *Good Knight Sleep Tight* by David Melling

Creative Planning in the EYFS • **Castles and dragons**

What to do

Read the story of *The Kiss That Missed* and talk together about where the kiss went after it missed the prince and floated out of the window. It arrived in the wild wood where the bears, wolves and owls lived. After that it floated up above the woods and into the clouds; right into a dragon's nostril! After tumbling through the trees the whole party returned through the landscape to the castle.

Explain to the children that they are going to draw a map on a large piece of paper showing the places in the story (the wood, the castle, the clouds) and illustrate it with pictures of the people or creatures that live there. They are then going to draw a sparkly silver line showing where the kiss began, where it travelled and where it finally ended.

Demonstrate to the children how to look in the book at the story and see where the kiss began. Draw the castle or even the bedroom of the prince, and draw the king blowing the kiss. Then refer back to the book and note where the kiss is next: in the wild wood. Draw the wild wood on the other side of the paper, adding in the pictures of owls, wolves and bears. Next draw the dragon, and above the dragon draw the clouds. Look back at the book to note what the landscape looked like and draw on the fields, hedges and roads where appropriate on the map. Finally read the book together once more and add in any extra detail (for example the snow) that the children think is important.

If this is to be a guided activity…

…then the children can work together with an adult to draw a map showing the journey of the kiss that missed. Ensure that they use the illustrations in the book as inspiration when drawing, and that they look carefully at the colours used (for example in the wild wood) to give atmosphere to their drawings. They could use collage material if required to add an extra dimension to their map (twig trees, cotton wool clouds and snow made from paper from a hole punch). Make it explicit that the route is circular and that the journey ends in the place it begins.

If this is to be an independent activity…

…then show the children where the paper and drawing materials are and explain that they can try this activity sometime this week. Provide copies of the pages from the book for the children to put in order before drawing so that they can see the journey in front of them. Try to ensure that they understand that the journey ends in the place it begins, so the silver swirly line denoting the route of the kiss will pass through different locations before joining up again at the castle.

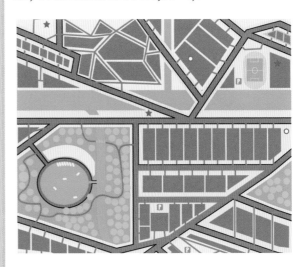

Knight journeys

Going on a dragon hunt!

The children will be going on a dragon hunt – choosing obstacles and acting it out together around the setting.

Resources

★ Flipchart

★ Variety of musical instruments

★ Pictures of different habitats and settings

Story books

★ *We're Going on a Bear Hunt* by Michael Rosen and Helen Oxenbury

Observation and assessment

Expressive arts and design	Expected statements (ELGs)
Exploring and using media and materials	Children sing songs, make music and dance, and experiment with ways of changing them. They safely use and explore a variety of materials, tools and techniques, experimenting with colour, design, texture, form and function.
Being imaginative	Children use what they have learnt about media and materials in original ways, thinking about uses and purposes. They represent their own ideas, thoughts and feelings through design and technology, art, music, dance, role-play and stories.

Key vocabulary

- over
- under
- around
- through
- sound
- instrument
- percussion
- setting
- habitat

What to do

Read and perform the well-known action rhyme 'Going on a bear hunt' with the children. Look at the book and talk about the pictures showing where the family walked and where they found the bear. Explain that the children are going to make up a rhyme called 'Going on a dragon hunt' and that they must think of different places to search for a dragon. Make a list on the flipchart of places to travel when leaving the castle; for example over the bridge, down the hill, under the trees, through the leaves, into the tower, up the stairs. Draw a little symbol for each of these places. Go through each place in turn, asking the children to imagine the sound that would be created when travelling, for example over the bridge (trip-trap, trip-trap), down the hill (run-roll, run-roll), under the trees (hide and seek! hide and seek!), through the leaves (scrunch kick! scrunch kick!), into the tower (creak-crurk, creak-crurk), up the stairs (shhh tippy-toe, shhh tippy-toe) until you get to 'aaagh! It's a dragon!' Repeat the journey, this time travelling backwards through the sound effects.

If this is to be a guided activity…

…then the children can work together in a group with an adult to create and act out their own version of 'Going on a dragon hunt'. Support some of the children in making a pictorial record of the journey and the obstacles encountered, and some of the other children to use the instruments to add sound effects to the story. Make a film or sound recording of the narrative to play for the children afterwards so that they can appraise what they have done. Encourage them to review it critically by discussing what they liked and also what they would do differently next time!

If this is to be an independent activity…

…then show the children where the collection of musical instruments is and explain that they are to imagine hunting for a dragon and making some music to represent what they experience. To begin, provide some laminated pictures of features such as bridges and mountains for the children to create sound effects for, but also provide paper and pencils for the children to draw their own features. Ensure that there is feedback time for the children who have done this activity to show their work to the other children and explain why they chose the sound effects they did.

To support or extend

To support, work with a small group of children outdoors to act out the bear hunt. When they understand the activity, change the creature to a dragon. As the adult, take advantage of the built environment when walking around and use it imaginatively to become a feature in the story. For example, walking over a drain cover could become 'Look! A dungeon! A deep, dark, dungeon!' A bush can become a jungle, a playhouse a castle and a quiet corner a cave! Take suggestions from the children and let them take turns to be the leader – it doesn't matter if they simply copy your ideas.

To extend, let the children choose a different creature to hunt for which lives in a different environment. For example, hunting for a creature that lived on a mountain may involve travelling over snow, climbing up rocks and riding on a mountain goat! To find a creature underwater may involve walking on sand, splashing in the waves, swimming in the sea and jumping on rocks. Make up a narrative and perform it as a group to the other children.

Ideas for interactive display

Provide a selection of musical percussion instruments on the display table for the children to investigate. Alongside these display laminated pictures of different story settings, including the moon, under the ocean, a children's party, the city and the countryside. Encourage the children to explore the instruments and make sounds and music to match the settings.

Parents and carers as partners

At home re-enact the story of 'Going on a bear hunt' by adding actions to the movements suggested in the story. Add some more of your own specific to where you walk, for example 'marching on the pavement', 'stamping on the stairs' or 'jumping over cracks'.

Kings and queens

An invitation to Sleeping Beauty's christening

The children will be reading the story and then writing invitations to the christening of Sleeping Beauty.

Observation and assessment

Literacy	Expected statements (ELGs)
Reading	Children read and understand simple sentences. They use phonic knowledge to decode regular words and read them aloud accurately. They also read some common irregular words. They demonstrate understanding when talking with others about what they have read.
Writing	Children use their phonic knowledge to write words in ways which match their spoken sounds. They also write some irregular common words. They write simple sentences which can be read by themselves and others. Some words are spelt correctly and others are phonetically plausible.

Key vocabulary

- invitation
- party
- wedding
- christening
- naming day
- ceremony
- celebration
- RSVP

Resources

★ Collection of invitations (used or new) including wedding, birthday, christening, party

★ Pieces of different coloured paper and card

★ Selection of envelopes

★ Magazines (wedding, baby, general)

Storybooks

★ *Sleeping Beauty* (many versions of this traditional tale are available)

★ *I want a party!* by Tony Ross (or any others in the Little Princess series)

To support, copy the basic frame of an invitation onto a piece of card. Ensure it simply says, 'To…Please come to my party At… On… From…' Let the children decide on the type of party and then cut pictures from the magazine to support their ideas. Stick these onto the card and support the children to write simple words onto the writing frame (names, day of the week etc.) to complete the invitations.

To extend help the children to write an RSVP card for an invitation you have supplied them with. Pretend they are in character as either a good or bad fairy and reply to the king and queen with their intention of attending the christening of Sleeping Beauty. Try to encourage them to ask a question or make a comment relevant to their character in the story.

What to do

Read *Sleeping Beauty* with the children. Explain that all the fairies in the story had been invited to a party to celebrate the princess Sleeping Beauty's christening. Talk to the children about parties and celebrations they have been invited to or have held for themselves – how did the people who came know where, when and what it was? Show the children the examples of different invitations. Draw their attention to the key parts of the invitation, including the need for the purpose, date, time, location, contact details and RSVP. Explain that RSVP is French for respondez, s'il vous plait and that it means please reply to say if you can come or not. Discuss why this is important. Look at a selection of invitations together – without reading the words can the children say for what type of event they are intended? How do they know – is it the colours used or the illustrations? Explain that some events have symbolic pictures, e.g. bells for a wedding, balloons for a party or teddy bears and dummies for baby events. Encourage all of the children to talk about events they have attended and those which they would like to attend. Show the children the word cards with the key features written on (date, time etc.) and rehearse reading them, to help the children with the next part of the activity – making an invitation of their own.

If this is to be a guided activity…

…then the children can work together with an adult to create their own invitation to an event. Decide together in a small group what the event will be, and then talk together about the theme of the invitations. Discuss appropriate colours, symbols and illustrations. Ensure that the children can remember the structural features of any invitation (date, time, location, purpose) and that these are relevant to the particular invitation they are creating.

If this is to be an independent activity…

…then show the children where the collection of small pieces of coloured paper and card are and encourage them to create their own invitation to an event of their own choosing. Let them select appropriate colours and cut further pictures from the magazines relevant to the theme and purpose of the invitation. Have the key features of invitations written out on cards for the children to copy if needed. Make a post box from a box, and allow the children to post their invitations to other children.

Ideas for interactive display

Display different invitations to different occasions. Ask the children to bring in different examples of invitations (birthday, wedding, christening or naming day, anniversary party) and put them out for the children to sort and order. Provide baskets so that they can be sorted accordingly – how do the children know that one is a birthday invitation and not a wedding invitation? What is similar and different? Put out small pieces of paper in different colours so that the children can create more invitations of their own to sort in the collection.

Parents and carers as partners

At home, make some invitations together for an event you are having at home. It could be a special occasion such as a birthday or christening or it could be something ordinary which you are making into something special, such as Friday tea or a visit to the park. Help your child with the structure, including the date and time, but encourage them to address it to the person they are inviting and also to sign it with their name.

Kings and queens

Stamps and coins – Royal maths

The children will be looking at stamps and coins which carry the royal portrait, and counting, adding and subtracting.

Andy Lidstone/Shutterstock.com

Observation and assessment

Mathematics	Expected statements (ELGs)
Number	Children count reliably with numbers from 1 to 20, place them in order and say which number is one more or one less than a given number. Using quantities and objects, they add and subtract two single-digit numbers and count on or back to find the answer. They solve problems, including doubling, halving and sharing.
Space, shape and measures	Children use everyday language to talk about size, weight, capacity, position, distance time and money to compare quantities and objects and to solve problems.

Key vocabulary

- stamp
- coin
- royal mint
- portrait
- profile
- amount
- denomination
- how much
- total
- sum
- add
- subtract
- take away

Resources

★ Selection of UK coins, at least one of each denomination

★ Range of UK stamps with amounts shown

★ Sticky labels

★ Homemade set of stamps from 1p to 10p

★ Whiteboard

Storybooks and non-fiction books

★ *The Great Pet Sale* by Mick Inkpen

What to do

Talk to the children about stamps and coins. Find out what they know about them – what is the same and what is different? Pass some around or display them on the whiteboard. Talk about the portrait of the Queen, explain that because she is the current monarch her portrait appears on most coins and stamps. Prior to Queen Elizabeth II it was her father, King George VI. If possible have a coin, stamp or photograph of him on a coin or stamp to show the children. Introduce the concept of coins and stamps being worth different amounts of money.

Read *The Great Pet Sale* by Mick Inkpen together. On each page draw the children's attention to the price label for each animal, explaining that the 'p' represents pence, which are amounts of 1ps. If possible make a list on a whiteboard. Following this, explain to the children that the royal palace is having a sale too! Ask the children to think of ten items that may be found in a palace or castle, for example throne, crown, jewellery, armour, sword, red carpet, gold cups, golden carriage, horse – let the children be as imaginative as they like! Assign each of these items a price from 1p to 10p, talking about the relative value of each where appropriate. Give each child a different amount of 1p coins for them to count. Read out the sale items and ask each child to stand up if the total amount of coins they have matches the price of the item. If the children are able to understand this concept then extend the idea to having enough pennies to buy more than one item – what pairs of items can they afford to buy? Can anyone buy three? How many pennies are needed to buy a horse and a carriage? How much more money would you need? Differentiate the questions according to the capability of the children.

If this is to be a guided activity…

…then the children can work together in a small group with an adult to hold and record a 'Royal sale'. Let each child draw a picture of a royal item onto a small label and add a price from 1p to 10p. Arrange these in order and give each child a handful of pennies. Help them to count their pennies carefully observing one to one correlation, and then talk together about what they could afford to buy. Following this, ask the children to 'buy' two items and calculate the total price. If required, support their recording of the mathematics onto a whiteboard, helping them to use appropriate symbols and to use mathematical vocabulary accurately.

If this is to be an independent activity…

…then show the children where the box of resources will be, and explain that they can try this activity sometime this week. Let them work in small groups to play shopping at the 'Royal sale', using coins to explore 'paying' and 'giving change'. Provide differently priced objects depending upon the capability of the children. If whiteboards are also provided then the children can record their emergent mathematics through pictures or their own symbols, or older children can write simple number sentences.

To support or extend

To support, have a selection of coins which are in our currency, several multiples of each. Give each child a set of coins and help them to look at the numbers on the coins and set them out in order of value. Some children will consider size to be most important so help them to look carefully for clues. Give each child a coin of the same value and look at the designs on the coins – are they all the same? Establish together what is the same each time and what is different.

To extend, use either coins or stamps worth 2p, 5p and 10p for counting in multiples and recording as repeated addition. Show the children how to put three 2p stamps in a line, for example, and to write 2p + 2p + 2p = 6p. Demonstrate counting in twos, or provide a laminated 100 square for the children to colour in the multiples of two. Extend this to 5p and 10p stamps where appropriate.

Ideas for interactive display

- Provide lots of real money for the children to sort, count, add, subtract and group. On the display have a selection of toys with price labels under 10p. Let the children play shopping and practise buying different items and combination of items using the coins.

- Similarly with stamps, have laminated versions of stamps worth different amounts to Blu tack onto different laminated envelopes. Write the total price on the back of the envelope and let the children investigate which stamps add up to that total.

Parents and carers as partners

At home let your child use and encounter money and coins frequently. Coins are used less and less in everyday life as plastic cards are more often used in transactions such as travel fares and shopping. Give your child a money box and let them 'earn' money for tasks such as pairing socks, putting away washing or tidying toys. These small denomination coins are excellent for counting, sorting, ordering, adding and grouping, and of course for spending on treats.

Kings and queens

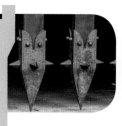

Portraits and thrones

The children will be creating a famous portrait gallery, making crowns and royal cardboard 'thrones'.

Observation and assessment

Understanding the world	Expected statements (ELGs)
People and communities	Children talk about past and present events in their own lives and the lives of family members. They know that other children don't always enjoy the same things and are sensitive to this.
The world	Children know about similarities and differences between themselves and others, and among families, communities and traditions.

Key vocabulary

- royal
- regal
- kind
- queen
- portrait
- image
- painting
- frame
- throne
- moulding

Resources

★ Gold paint

★ Gold paper and ribbons

★ Cardboard cereal boxes

★ Pasta shapes

★ PVA glue

★ Examples of famous royal portraits

★ Selection of regal furnishings, including drapes, cloaks, faux fur rugs, ribbon etc.

★ Pegs, chairs and a quiet corner

Storybooks

★ *I want a sister!* by Tony Ross (or any others in the Little Princess series)

★ *Portraits* (First Discovery/Art) by Claude Delafosse and Tony Ross

What to do

Explain that many years ago, before there were cameras and methods of recording images the only way of remembering what someone looked like was to draw or paint their picture. Show the children a selection of royal portraits, including Henry VIII and more recent kings and queens. Talk about how the children can tell they are famous people – what are they wearing? Are they standing or sitting? Can you see their entire body or just their head and shoulders? Look at the frames of the paintings – why are they gold coloured and not plain wood? Explain to the children that they are going to make a frame for a royal portrait and decorate it with gold paint. Show them how to cut up a cereal box to make a cardboard frame. If you leave the box intact and simply cut out a rectangle on the front panel then different portraits can be slid inside the box frame. Using a variety of dried pasta shapes lay out a pattern onto the 'frame' of the box, gluing it down with lots of PVA glue to ensure it stays stuck when lifted vertically. Leave it to dry at least overnight until firmly glued then paint the entire box with gold paint. The pasta frame will look like gilded mouldings and the children can paint portraits of themselves or others as kings and queens, to be displayed in a royal portrait gallery.

If this is to be a guided activity…

…then the children can work together with an adult to build some large cardboard thrones for the king and queen to sit on whilst they are posing for their royal portrait. Using a regular child's chair, cut out an elaborate back for the chair which is taller than a seated child. Paint this in gold paint or wrap it in gold paper or ribbon, along with the chair legs and seat. Drape some regal looking materials about the 'throne' (for example red velvet, faux fur rugs etc.) and invite a child to sit on it as if posed for a portrait. The remaining children can sketch the child or take a photograph of them, but remind the children of the initial learning point; that in the past, prior to cameras, portraits were painted instead.

If this is to be an independent activity…

…then show the children where the selection of objects are and explain that they can try this activity sometime this week. Provide a selection of cloths, cloaks, drapes, pegs, faux fur rugs and collars, crowns, elaborate paste jewellery and other royal accoutrement. Tell the children that they are going to create a corner of the palace or castle which is where the king and queen will sit for their royal portrait. Let the children enjoy draping the chairs and furniture in fabric and pegging it securely, laying down royal rugs and hanging royal ribbon! They will love to build a 'den' in this way. Complete the role-play by allowing them to dress themselves and each other in royal clothes and jewellery, taking turns to sit for a portrait!

To support or extend

To support, have a selection of pasta shapes and begin a pattern using two or three varieties for the children to continue. When complete help them to paint it liberally with gold paint. They could either create their own portrait to put in the frame or they could cut out pictures of the current royal family to use. Show them that a portrait is usually formally posed for, and that it is unlikely that a royal portrait would show a person walking about in a town, for example.

To extend, explain that some royal or important people would include in their portraits objects which were important to them or that showed their wealth to other people. Talk together about what a king or queen might want people to see, for example a crown, jewellery, furs, musical instruments or pens and quills. Provide a selection of objects and invite the children to bring in more of their own. Let the children pose for a royal portrait; the other children could draw them or even take their photograph as a modern equivalent.

Ideas for interactive display

Provide pictures of different members of the royal family at different times in their life, for example when they were babies, children, when they were married and in older age. Have labels for them so that the children know who they are, such as Queen Elizabeth II, Prince Phillip, Prince William and the Duchess of Cambridge, Prince Harry. Help the children to match the photographs to the labels. They can extend this further by ordering several photographs of the Queen, for example, in the order her age, by looking at the clothes she wore as a child and at the style of the photographs.

William Attard McCarthy/Shutterstock.com

Parents and carers as partners

At home, look at the people in your family and try to get a photograph of each. Lay these out so that your child can talk about them and begin to arrange them in a rough family tree. Begin with your child, and alongside them put any pictures of brothers and sisters. Above this put the parents and carers generation, and above this the child's grandparents. Many children are fascinated by the idea that their own parents have parents too!

Kings and queens

Royal songs

The children will be singing and performing songs with a royal theme.

Resources

★ Songs such as Old King Cole/Sing a Song of Sixpence/Pussy Cat Pussy Cat Where Have You Been?/Humpty Dumpty/Grand Old Duke of York

★ Props related to these popular rhymes, including cat, star, moon, sheep, little boy etc.

★ Selection of percussion or homemade instruments

★ Whiteboard

Storybooks and non-fiction books

★ *Pat-a-cake, Make and Shake* by Sue Nicholls

★ Books containing nursery rhymes, poems and songs

Observation and assessment

Expressive arts and design	Expected statements (ELGs)
Exploring and using media and materials	Children sing songs, make music and dance, and experiment with ways of changing them.
Being imaginative	They represent their own ideas, thoughts and feelings through design and technology, art, music, dance, role-play and stories.

Key vocabulary

- king
- queen
- duke
- royal
- London
- rhyme
- rhythm
- song
- sound

What to do

Explain to the children that they are going to learn some nursery rhymes with actions and perform them to the other children in the setting. Nursery rhymes were frequently made up to talk about the royal events of the day and as a result there are many with a royal theme. The nursery rhymes will all have a royal theme, and the children can play instruments along with the songs to add percussive sound effects. If instruments are in short supply then make some of your own from scrap materials – there are many good ideas in the Sue Nicholls book listed. Sing a selection of the nursery rhymes listed above, adding any more that the children think of. To extend the more able children have the words displayed on a poster or on the whiteboard so that they can read along whilst they sing. Look at the words and the rhythm of the rhymes – if you are saying them together and then you stop before the end of the line, can the children suggest the missing word? If the children think of another rhyming word is it possible to make up a silly rhyme of their own? When you have a verse that the children are all able to recite with confidence and expression, talk to the children about adding sound effects from the instruments available. Voices may be more suited to create some sounds (for example cats talking, mice squeaking in fright!) but the children will have some very imaginative ideas about others! When they are satisfied with their soundtrack let them perform it to another group of children. Appraise it together, asking if the sound effects enhanced the telling of the story rhyme or not. If appropriate, annotate the large written poem with pictures, signs and symbols to help them to remember what and when to play or make a sound. This attempt at an early musical score will support the children in reading information in a different way to text and numbers.

If this is to be a guided activity…

…then the children can work together in a group with an adult to create a performance of a royal rhyme. Learn to speak together in order to recite it with feeling and expression before exploring the percussion instruments with a view to providing a soundtrack to the events in the rhyme. For example, in Sing a Song of Sixpence they could create jingling coins for the sixpences, some whistling birdsong for the blackbirds and baking noises for the pie! Let the children be as imaginative as possible – the songs may sound crazy but it will make sense to them and help them to remember the words in the correct order.

If this is to be an independent activity…

…then show the children where the instruments are and explain that they can try this activity sometime this week. If there are few instruments provide junk modelling materials so the children can make their own. Have laminated cards with the words and pictures to different rhymes on, or have some pre-recorded onto a device that the children can listen to independently. Allow them to devise and perform a musical score appropriate to the rhyme chosen. If possible, record this again for other children to listen to and comment upon.

To support or extend

To support, use a single verse of a short rhyme familiar to the children to add instruments to. Have a small selection of instruments for the children to explore first, playing each one and talking about what it sounds like. Recite the rhyme again and ask very structured questions, such as, 'Do we have something that would make a jingling sound? How could we make a knocking sound?' Perform the rhyme again using the instruments for other children to listen to and appraise.

To extend, have a selection of props for nursery rhymes in a lucky dip bag. Let the children pull one out (for example a character mask, a particular hat, a cat, a star, a sheep etc.) and think of a rhyme linked to that item. There may be more than one and this will promote discussion about which to choose. Let the children then perform that rhyme, or have a CD player with a selection of rhymes on for them to play and listen to.

Ideas for interactive display

Provide a selection of props which are linked to different nursery rhymes. Some will overlap with others; for example, there are cats in more than one, and coins. Have a picture card which will identify the nursery rhyme and some hoops, so that the children can group the matching objects and cards together.

Parents and carers as partners

At home, sing nursery rhymes together frequently, particularly those which have actions to them. The tune and the repetitive, rhythmic nature will help your child to speak and read later on. If you are unsure of many rhymes there are lots of CDs which you can buy with music and rhymes – some come with a book. These are great to play in the car, if you can stand it!

A grand banquet!

Royal feast

The final week of the topic is an opportunity to invite parents and carers into the setting to share some of the activities in which the children have been involved over the preceeding five weeks.

Tickell stated in her review that,

> 'Where parents and carers are actively encouraged to participate confidently in their children's learning and healthy development, the outcomes for children will be at their best'

It is crucial that parents and carers are involved and feel able to support their children at every stage of development. This final week is, therefore, a time for the children to celebrate their successes, perform some of their new skills for their families to see and for parents and carers to be involved in their learning.

In the week building up to inviting the parents and carers into the setting the children can be involved in making invitations, decorations, food and practising songs, drama and dances to share on the special day.

The actual event can be really flexible in length, style and amount of parental involvement. Depending on the setting and the number of children involved it is possible to make this event an hour or a day long, or you may need to repeat it for two different cohorts of children. It could simply be an open style morning or afternoon for people to drop in, to look at things the children have made, or be a mini concert, where the children can perform dances, sing songs for the parents and afterwards share food the children have produced.

Whatever the design, the purpose is to share some of the activities and crafts the children have been involved in, and to celebrate the topic of castles and dragons.

Listed opposite are ideas for celebration linked to each of the seven areas of learning, along with some ideas for parental involvement and understanding. The detailed expected ELG is also noted again here as a reminder of the expected level of attainment and understanding.

These are just some of the possible ideas – have fun, be creative and do whatever works for you and your children!

Ideas for a grand banquet

- Make invitations, cards and decorations – invitations to a royal feast; flags, thrones and bunting; prince, princess and dragon masks, knight's armour, or golden jewelled crowns to wear;

- Decorate the setting with some of the artwork produced – display the coats of arms, moving armour and life sized knight collage; have a castle art corner and display the box model and cereal castles;

- Eat special food – make some royal crustless sandwiches to share with the parents and carers, or bake some dragon biscuits dipped in green icing;

- Dress up in special clothing – allow the children to wear their best party clothes to be young princes and princesses, or wear knight or dragon costumes; decorate the children's faces with coats of arms painted onto their cheeks;

- Play party games – go on a grand dragon hunt together around the setting; sing the royal songs like 'Sing a song of sixpence' and 'Pussy cat, pussy cat'; go on an adventure through an obstacle course whilst on a knight's journey.

Opportunities within Literacy

Aspect	Expected statements (ELGs)
Reading	Children read and understand simple sentences. They use phonic knowledge to decode regular words and read them aloud accurately. They also read some common irregular words. They demonstrate understanding when talking with others about what they have read.
Writing	Children use their phonic knowledge to write words in ways which match their spoken sounds. They also write some irregular common words. They write simple sentences which can be read by themselves and others. Some words are spelt correctly and others are phonetically plausible.

Most parents and carers are used to and comfortable with sharing books with children, as it is something that they have enjoyed regularly at home as their child has grown up. It's therefore a good idea to set up a corner of the setting with cushions, low tables and chairs to invite adults to sit quietly with the children reading, talking and listening. Put out a selection of books related to the topic, particularly including books that the children have seen before and which they have enjoyed in the setting. Include both fiction and non-fiction to appeal to a wide range of children and adults, and also include dual language texts. The children will relish being the expert when sharing the books with their parent or carer, and it gives a little quiet time to those finding the celebration a little busy.

Put out a writing area with a variety of suitable materials – include sticky labels, coloured sticky notes, postcards, envelopes, folded pieces of paper, lined, squared and dotted paper, old birthday or Christmas cards, old diaries and calendars and anything else the children would like to write upon! Include a mixture of pens, pencils and crayons. In this area also include blank invitations, picture holiday postcards, holiday travel brochures and comics and magazines to colour, cut and stick – the children and adults can have fun writing to each other and making postcards or invitations. Include some of the royal stamps created by the children, and provide blank sticky labels so that they can make more. Children then see writing as having a purpose. If there are a variety of materials which are easily found in a home setting it may give ideas to the adults to encourage them to provide similar writing opportunities at home.

Opportunities within Mathematics

Aspect	Expected statements (ELGs)
Numbers	Children count reliably with numbers from 1 to 20, place them in order and say which number is one more or one less than a given number. Using quantities and objects, they add and subtract two single-digit numbers and count on or back to find the answer. They solve problems, including doubling, halving and sharing.
Space, shape and measures	Children use everyday language to talk about size, weight, capacity, position, distance, time and money to compare quantities and objects and to solve problems. They recognise, create and describe patterns. They explore characteristics of everyday objects and shapes and use mathematical language to describe them.

Let the children prepare for the adults visiting the setting by working out how many things will be needed for the banquet: how many chairs altogether; how many around each table; how many cups or plates are needed? Setting the tables: have we enough; how many more; are they the same/equal? Extend this idea to the preparation of food when weighing or measuring quantities for making biscuits or when buttering and cutting bread for sandwiches.

Have a basket of sixpences (from Sing a Song of Sixpence) or coins made by the children for the parents to 'spend' when they are buying an item for the banquet – can they

help the children to count accurately? Put out the dice dragons games and the dragon's tail and Rapunzel's hair board games made by the children for the visitors to play. Provide a box of beads for the children to use when making royal jewellery by threading or by gluing onto a crown shape – can they make a symmetrical or repeating pattern?

These ideas are easily replicated at home, and the parents and carers can see how easy it is to provide simple mathematical activities at home without any special books or mathematical equipment.

Opportunities within Understanding the world

Aspect	Expected statements (ELGs)
People and communities	Children talk about past and present events in their own lives and in the lives of family members. They know that other children don't always enjoy the same things, and are sensitive to this. They know about similarities and differences between themselves and others, and among families, communities and traditions.
The world	Children know about similarities and differences in relation to places, objects, materials and living things. They talk about the features of their own immediate environment and how environments might vary from one another. They make observations of animals and plants and explain why some things occur, and talk about changes.
Technology	Children recognise that a range of technology is used in places such as homes and schools. They select and use technology for particular purposes.

Make a display of the catapults (trebuchet) made by the children in week 2. The children will love showing how they work and the parents and carers may become quite competitive themselves investigating them!

The use of ICT in the setting may be the most surprising to the parent and carer visitors. Ensure the computers and whiteboard are on (if you have them), digital cameras and voice recorders are available to use and toys such as programmable toys and pretend telephones and ovens are out for the children to show to the adults. Many parents and carers will believe that ICT relates only to computers: this is an opportunity to show them that technology includes the common objects in their own home. Provide a facility for the children to play the sound recordings they have made of their narratives, including those of the Knight's Walk and Going on a dragon hunt.

A very simple but effective idea is to put all the photographs you have taken over the previous five weeks on as a slideshow – the children will love pointing themselves out, it is good evidence of the type of activities the children have been involved in and it will naturally prompt talk, listening and laughter.

Opportunities within Expressive arts and design

Aspect	Expected statements (ELGs)
Exploring and using media and materials	Children sing songs, make music and dance, and experiment with ways of changing them. They safely use and explore a variety of materials, tools and techniques, experimenting with colour, design, texture, form and function.
Being imaginative	Children use what they have learnt about media and materials in original ways, thinking about uses and purposes. They represent their own ideas, thoughts and feelings through design and technology, art, music, dance, role-play and stories.

Have an area set out as a place where adults and children can work together to produce decorations and artwork relevant to the topics looked at over the preceding five weeks. Provide bricks and boxes for the children to build 3D castles and houses; put the chalks outside for the children to draw mazes and routes on the ground; or provide brushes and water for the children to 'write' with outside on the floor. Simple pictures to colour (e.g. pictures of castles, dragons, knights in armour or princes and princesses) is also a popular activity which many adults recognise, and may choose to sit alongside children and participate in without any fear of 'doing it wrong'.

If your setting allows for it, prepare an area with some musical instruments (include both those made by the children and existing ones) and possibly a CD player with some exciting adventurous music. Let the children play the CD and investigate playing the instruments alongside. This activity works well outdoors, as there is more space for the children to creep, stamp and explore with the instruments whilst hunting for dragons. The increased space may also enable children to feel 'free' and you may find that they initiate an entire royal parade, making music and marching in time to the music! If you extend their opportunities by also providing crowns, helmets, masks, coloured scarves, flags and banners they are also more likely to develop characters within the music and begin to role play quite naturally. Parents and carers can see from this that expensive character fancy dress sets are not necessary – with only a couple of old hats and scarves they can provide valuable opportunities at home for dressing up and firing the imagination of their child.

Opportunities within Communication and language

Aspect	Expected statements (ELGs)
Listening and attention	Children listen attentively in a range of situations. They listen to stories, accurately anticipating key events and respond to what they hear with relevant comments, questions or actions. They give their attention to what others say and respond appropriately, while engaged in another activity.
Understanding	Children follow instructions involving several ideas or actions. They answer 'how' and 'why' questions about their experiences and in response to stories or events.
Speaking	Children express themselves effectively, showing awareness of listeners' needs. They use past, present and future forms accurately when talking about events that have happened or are to happen in the future. They develop their own narratives and explanations by connecting ideas or events.

For some children who can find the setting a little overwhelming sharing their activities and successes with a familiar adult can be reassuring. They appreciate the time to be the expert, talking to their parent or carer about their daily activities and routines without the pressure to chat to a stranger or in front of others. For the practitioner in the setting this is also an ideal opportunity to listen quietly and unobtrusively to the child's conversation with others – it may be the first time you have heard the child speak!

Opportunities within Physical development

Aspect	Expected statements (ELGs)
Moving and handling	Children show good control and co-ordination in large and small movements. They move confidently in a range of ways, safely negotiating space. They handle equipment and tools effectively, including pencils for writing.
Health and self-care	Children know the importance for good health of physical exercise, and a healthy diet, and talk about ways to keep healthy and safe. They manage their own basic hygiene and personal needs successfully, including dressing and going to the toilet independently.

This can link quite closely with the music and movement idea in Expressive arts and design where the children can move confidently and with control around the outdoor environment. It is useful for the parents and carers to note that young children need to have opportunities for physical play or movement several times a day, whether it is walking to school or running around the local park or garden.

Provide ropes, canes and boxes for the children to plan out maps, routes and mazes and encourage them to give the adults directions in order for them to complete the task and find the dragon or treasure.

There are many activities which encourage fine motor skills, including threading beads to make royal jewellery; making flag or coats of arms patterns with coloured pegs and peg boards; building castles with construction or using pencils to trace, write, draw and colour. Parents can extend this at home very simply without any special equipment, for example by threading penne pasta onto string to make jewellery, using clothes pegs to hang out the washing; playing with small construction (e.g.

Lego) or small world (e.g. a doll's house) or cutting pieces of baking paper for children to place over the pictures in their colouring book to use as a cheap alternative to tracing paper. It is vital that parents recognise these pre-writing skills as crucial in a child's fine motor development.

To promote good health and self-care it is useful to have a large display where the children (but more importantly, the parents and carers) can see it, showing which children can achieve such things as using the toilet independently, washing their hands, putting on their own coat or fastening their own shoes. Maybe have small photographs of each child, and when they have achieved the target then their photograph is moved onto, for example, a large outline of a coat. These can be themed to match the topic, e.g. 'I can put on my armour by myself.' The children in the setting will then be very aware of what they need to do, and will take this information home in the form of pester power – quickly learning how to perform the skill! Sometimes parents and carers do not realise what is necessary for their child to become more independent.

Opportunities within Personal, social and emotional development

Aspect	Expected statements (ELGs)
Self-confidence and self-awareness	Children are confident to try new activities, and say why they like some activities more than others. They are confident to speak in a familiar group, will talk about their ideas, and will choose the resources they need for their chosen activities. They say when they do or don't need help.
Managing feelings and behaviour	Children talk about how they and others show feelings, talk about their own and others' behaviour, and its consequences, and know that some behaviour is unacceptable. They work as part of a group or class, and understand and follow the rules. They adjust their behaviour to different situations, and take changes of routine in their stride.
Making relationships	Children play co-operatively, taking turns with others. They take account of one another's ideas about how to organise their activity. They show sensitivity to others' needs and feelings, and form positive relationships with adults and other children.

Within the six week topic block there are continual opportunities for children to demonstrate their development in the aspect of PSED. Each activity throughout the previous weeks requires children to work together, co-operate, talk about their ideas, choose resources and form positive relationships with others. This final opportunity for celebration allows the children to show that this positive behaviour is embedded, as the key skill of 'adjusting their behaviour to different situations and taking changes in routine in their stride' is certainly tested during this busy week.

Make a note of any children who have struggled with certain aspects of PSED and ensure that they are prepared for this change in routine: pair them with a particular friend for security; provide them with a quiet space (e.g. a tent, a book corner, even another room in the setting with another group) to which they can escape when it becomes too much; give them a key responsibility to prevent idle hands (such as handing out biscuits to adults, collecting empty cups or even tidying pencils and putting away chairs) or simply ensure that they are your 'special helper' and that they are to stay with you throughout the event. This way you are building on the personal, social and emotional capabilities of your children and allowing them to develop further within a safe and structured environment.

Ensure most importantly that parents and carers understand the uniqueness of each child. Measuring their child's attainment, progress and temperament against that of another child is of no benefit whatsoever. A child who feels loved, supported and a valuable member of their early years community will grow and develop into an adult that is able to love and support others, and more importantly will be a valuable member of any community they choose to belong to throughout the rest of their life.

Observation record: Characteristics of Effective Learning

Name: _____   DoB: _____

Characteristics	Date	Activity observed	Evidence (What did you see?)
Playing and Exploring • Finding out and exploring • Playing with what they know • Being willing to 'have a go'			
Through active learning • Being involved and concentrating • Keeping trying • Enjoying achieving what they set out to do			
By creating and thinking critically • Having their own ideas • Making links • Choosing ways to do things			

Creative Planning in the EYFS © Lucy Peet

Group record sheet for Communication and language (**prime**) and Literacy (**specific**)

Date completed _____

Children's names	Communication and language (prime)									Literacy (specific)							
	Listening and attention			Understanding			Speaking			Reading				Writing			

Group record sheet for **prime** areas of learning (Personal, social and emotional development and Physical development)   Date completed

Children's names	Personal, social and emotional development (prime)									Physical development (prime)						
	Self-confidence and self-awareness			Managing feelings and behaviour			Making relationships			Moving and handling			Health and self-care			

Group record sheet for **specific** area of learning (Mathematics)

Date completed _____

Children's names	Mathematics (specific)					Comments
	Numbers			Shape, space and measures		

Children's names	Understanding the world (specific)									Expressive arts and design (specific)					
	People and communities			The world			Technology			Exploring and using media and materials			Being imaginative		

Planning overview: Castles and dragons (6 weeks)

Week	Main topic and activities	ELGs covered from specific areas of learning				
		Literacy including some communication and language	Mathematics	Understanding the world	Expressive arts and design	
1	**Castles and houses** • Rapunzel, Rapunzel • Box model castles • Traditional homes from around the world • Cereal castles	**Reading and listening to the story of Rapunzel and retelling it using props, including a lolly stick character with yellow ribbon hair.** Children listen attentively in a range of situations. They listen to stories, accurately anticipating key events and respond to what they hear with relevant comments, questions or actions. They use past, present and future forms accurately when talking about events that have happened or are to happen in the future. They develop their own narratives and explanations by connecting ideas or events.	**Making a castle from 3D box models, and adding moving parts such as drawbridge and portcullis.** Children use everyday language to talk about size, weight, capacity, position, distance, time and money to compare quantities and objects and to solve problems. They recognise, create and describe patterns. They explore characteristics of everyday objects and shapes and use mathematical language to describe them.	**Looking at castles, houses and homes from around the world, and building a collage of these on a large world map.** Children talk about past and present events in their own lives and the lives of family members. They know about similarities and differences between themselves and others, and among families, communities and traditions.	**Using mosaic paper squares and square breakfast cereal to build a crenelated castle on plain paper, adding towers and turrets from paper shapes** They safely use and explore a variety of materials, tools and techniques, experimenting with colour, design, texture, form and function. Children use what they have learnt about media and materials in original ways, thinking about uses and purposes. They represent their own ideas, thoughts and feelings through design and technology, art, music, dance, role-play and stories.	
2	**Armour and battles** • Coat of arms • Clothes peg catapult! • Moving armour • Life-sized knight collage	**Making a personal coat of arms using initial letters in their name.** Children listen attentively in a range of situations. They listen to stories, accurately anticipating key events and respond to what they hear with relevant comments, questions or actions. Children follow instructions involving several ideas or actions. Children use their phonic knowledge to write words in ways which match their spoken sounds. They also write some irregular common words. Some words are spelt correctly and others are phonetically plausible.	**Building a catapult from clothes pegs and a spoon, and measuring the distance an object is flung.** Children count reliably with numbers from 1 to 20, place them in order and say which number is one more or one less than a given number. Children use everyday language to talk about size, weight, capacity, position, distance, time and money to compare quantities and objects and to solve problems. They explore characteristics of everyday objects and shapes and use mathematical language to describe them.	**Making some moving armour – a headband with visor.** Children know about similarities and differences in relation to places, objects, materials and living things. Children recognise that a range of technology is used in places such as homes and schools. They select and use technology for particular purposes.	**Using shiny collage to make a life-sized knight in armour.** They safely use and explore a variety of materials, tools and techniques, experimenting with colour, design, texture, form and function. Children use what they have learnt about media and materials in original ways, thinking about uses and purposes.	

Planning overview: Castles and dragons (6 weeks)

Week	Main topic and activities	ELGs covered from specific areas of learning			
		Literacy — including some communication and language	Mathematics	Understanding the world	Expressive arts and design
3	**Dangerous dragons!** · Dragon design · Dice dragons · Dragon: WANTED! · Dragon's tail board game	Drawing and labelling a dragon of their own design, explaining their chosen features. They answer 'how' and 'why' questions about their experiences and in response to stories or events. Children use their phonic knowledge to write words in ways which match their spoken sounds. They also write some irregular common words. They write simple sentences which can be read by themselves and others. Some words are spelt correctly and others are phonetically plausible.	Building a dragon by rolling dice and adding numbered body parts. Children count reliably with numbers from 1 to 20, place them in order and say which number is one more or one less than a given number. Using quantities and objects, they add and subtract two single-digit numbers and count on or back to find the answer.	Talking about which jobs would be suitable for a dragon, and writing a job advert. They know about similarities and differences between themselves and others, and among families, communities and traditions. Children know about similarities and differences in relation to places, objects, materials and living things. They make observations of animals and plants and explain why some things occur, and talk about changes.	Making a board game based upon snakes and ladders; climbing up Rapunzel's hair and sliding down a dragon's tail. They safely use and explore a variety of materials, tools and techniques, experimenting with colour, design, texture, form and function. Children use what they have learnt about media and materials in original ways, thinking about uses and purposes. They represent their own ideas, thoughts and feelings through design and technology, art, music, dance, role-play and stories.
4	**Knight journeys** · A knight's walk · Roads and mazes · Follow the journey · Going on a dragon hunt!	Retelling Rosie's Walk as the journey of a knight, using over, under, past and through. They listen to stories, accurately anticipating key events and respond to what they hear with relevant comments, questions or actions. Children follow instructions involving several ideas or actions. Children express themselves effectively, showing awareness of listeners' needs. They use past, present and future forms accurately when talking about events that have happened or are to happen in the future. They develop their own narratives and explanations by connecting ideas or events.	Looking at roads, including direction, length, straight, curved, and routes through mazes. Children use everyday language to talk about size, weight, capacity, position, distance, time and money to compare quantities and objects and to solve problems. They recognise, create and describe patterns.	Drawing on a map of the castle the route of 'the kiss that missed' in a story. Children know about similarities and differences in relation to places, objects, materials and living things. They talk about the features of their own immediate environment and how environments might vary from one another.	Going on a dragon hunt – choosing obstacles and acting it out together around the setting. Children sing songs, make music and dance, and experiment with ways of changing them. They safely use and explore a variety of materials, tools and techniques, experimenting with colour, design, texture, form and function. Children use what they have learnt about media and materials in original ways, thinking about uses and purposes. They represent their own ideas, thoughts and feelings through design and technology, art, music, dance, role-play and stories.

Creative Planning in the EYFS © Lucy Peet

Planning overview: Castles and dragons (6 weeks)

Week	Main topic and activities	ELGs covered from specific areas of learning			
		Literacy including some communication and language	Mathematics	Understanding the world	Expressive arts and design
5	**Kings, queens, princes and princesses** • An invitation to Sleeping Beauty's christening • Stamps and coins – Royal maths • Portraits and thrones • Royal songs	Reading the story then writing invitations to the christening of Sleeping Beauty. Children read and understand simple sentences. They use phonic knowledge to decode regular words and read them aloud accurately. They also read some common irregular words. They demonstrate understanding when talking with others about what they have read. Children use their phonic knowledge to write words in ways which match their spoken sounds. They also write some irregular common words. They write simple sentences which can be read by themselves and others. Some words are spelt correctly and others are phonetically plausible.	Looking at stamps and coins which carry the royal portrait and counting, adding and subtracting. Children count reliably with numbers from 1 to 20, place them in order and say which number is one more or one less than a given number. Using quantities and objects, they add and subtract two single-digit numbers and count on or back to find the answer. They solve problems, including doubling, halving and sharing. Children use everyday language to talk about size, weight, capacity, position, distance, time and money to compare quantities and objects and to solve problems.	Creating a famous portrait gallery, making crowns and royal cardboard 'thrones.' Children talk about past and present events in their own lives and the lives of family members. They know that other children don't always enjoy the same things and are sensitive to this. Children know about similarities and differences between themselves and others, and among families, communities and traditions.	Singing and performing songs with a royal theme. Children sing songs, make music and dance, and experiment with ways of changing them. They represent their own ideas, thoughts and feelings through design and technology, art, music, dance, role-play and stories.
6	**A grand banquet!**	Ideas to share with parents and carers			